Building Accessible Web Experiences with AI

Building Accessible Web Experiences with AI

Ashok Kumar Yadav

CONTENTS

Redefining Accessibility in the Age of AI

1.1 The Expanding Definition of Accessibility

For much of the web's early history, accessibility was narrowly interpreted as making a page readable by a screen reader. In truth, accessibility encompasses far more: it is the discipline of ensuring that every individual—regardless of ability, context, or device—can perceive, understand, navigate, and interact with digital content effectively.

Today, this concept extends beyond permanent disabilities. It includes temporary impairments (such as a broken wrist or screen glare), situational constraints (like poor connectivity or noisy environments), and even cognitive overload caused by complex interfaces. Accessibility has evolved into a lens through which resilience, inclusivity, and usability are measured.

When we discuss the role of AI in accessibility, we are fundamentally asking a deeper question: how can intelligent systems reduce friction between human intention and digital interaction?

1.2 The Business and Ethical Imperative

Accessibility is not charity—it is strategy. Globally, over 1.3 billion people live with some form of disability (WHO, 2023)—nearly one in six people. When a website or product fails to meet accessibility standards, it excludes not just a demographic—it excludes a significant share of potential customers, employees, and advocates.

Legal frameworks such as the Equality Act (UK), ADA (US), and EN 301 549 (EU) have established accessibility as a civil right. Yet compliance alone represents only the baseline—it is the floor, not the ceiling.

The ethical question remains clear: Should access to knowledge, commerce, and community depend on one's ability to see, hear, or manipulate a mouse? From that perspective, AI becomes not merely a tool for automation but a means to scale empathy through computation.

1.3 The Limits of Manual Accessibility

For more than two decades, accessibility auditing has relied heavily on checklists—WCAG 2.0, 2.1, and now 2.2. Developers run tools like Lighthouse or axe-core, adjust color contrast, add ARIA attributes, and often consider the job done.

However, studies from Deque Systems and WebAIM continue to show that over 96% of homepages still contain detectable WCAG violations. The reasons are multifaceted:

- **Scale:** large organizations may have thousands of templates and variants; manual testing cannot scale effectively.
- **Complexity:** dynamic components such as modals, carousels, and chatbots introduce interaction patterns beyond the reach of static rule-based tools.
- **Human error:** accessibility regressions frequently reappear with new releases.
- **Contextual gaps:** tools can flag missing alt text, but not whether that text conveys the right meaning.

This is where AI enters the picture—not to replace human judgment, but to fill the gaps that humans alone cannot efficiently address.

1.4 Accessibility as an Engineering Discipline

Accessibility was once a final-stage QA task—checked just before launch. Modern engineering, however, treats accessibility as a system property akin to performance, security, or reliability.

To achieve this, accessibility must be:

- **Observable:** with telemetry and metrics integrated into CI/CD pipelines.
- **Automated:** core WCAG checks enforced during builds and deployments.
- **Continuous:** models improving over time through user behavior data.
- **Integrated:** AI-driven agents suggesting improvements in real time.

In short, accessibility is moving from manual compliance to adaptive intelligence. Imagine an AI service trained on user interaction data that dynamically adjusts focus order or provides contextual cues when confusion is detected—that is accessibility as a living, evolving system.

1.5 AI as a Bridge, Not a Shortcut

AI can automate many accessibility tasks—generating alt text, identifying low contrast, or flagging inaccessible components. However, automation without understanding can easily produce confident inaccuracy.

For instance, a model might describe an image of a runner simply as "person running," while the meaningful context could be "a blind athlete finishing a marathon." Both are technically correct; only one conveys true human significance.

Therefore, AI should augment, not replace, accessibility expertise. Human oversight remains essential for ensuring nuance, empathy, and accuracy. The future lies in collaboration: AI handles the repeatable; humans handle the responsible.

1.6 The Economics of Inclusion

Accessibility once struggled under the question, "What's the ROI?" AI is rapidly transforming that equation.

- Automated testing and remediation dramatically reduce cost and time-to-fix.
- Predictive analytics highlight where regressions are likely to occur, enabling proactive prevention.
- AI-driven personalization adjusts reading levels, contrast, or interface behavior in real time—enhancing satisfaction for all users.

Organizations adopting AI-enabled accessibility aren't merely compliant—they are more competitive. Inclusive design expands markets, lowers legal risk, and strengthens brand trust. When powered by AI, accessibility evolves from an obligation into a strategic advantage.

1.7 The Legal and Standards Landscape

The Web Content Accessibility Guidelines (WCAG) remain the foundation of global digital accessibility. WCAG 2.2 reinforces the four core principles—Perceivable, Operable, Understandable, and Robust (POUR).

Looking ahead, WCAG 3.0 ("Silver") introduces outcome-based scoring that reflects adaptive technologies and user context. This marks a shift from static compliance checklists to context-aware conformance models—aligned with AI-driven personalization.

Governments and regulators are following suit. The European Accessibility Act (2025) explicitly acknowledges AI-based assistive technologies, moving the conversation beyond compliance toward capability.

1.8 Real-World Accessibility Gaps

Despite technological advances, common accessibility failures remain:

- Missing or meaningless alt text.
- Keyboard traps within modals or navigation menus.
- Low color contrast (below WCAG AA 4.5:1).
- Misused ARIA roles causing confusion for screen readers.
- Broken focus management in single-page applications.
- Non-descriptive link text (for example, "Click here").

AI can detect many of these at scale—but not intent. It may suggest a role attribute but cannot determine whether behavior matches semantics. The most effective accessibility strategy therefore combines machine precision with human insight.

1.9 Accessibility as User Experience

Accessibility is not separate from design—it *is* design. Interfaces built with inclusivity in mind inherently enhance usability for everyone: faster load times, clearer hierarchy, and improved SEO.

AI can amplify these universal benefits:

- Speech-to-text tools aid users with hearing impairments and anyone in noisy environments.

- Text simplification models assist neurodiverse users while improving readability for non-native speakers.
- Automated captions benefit not only accessibility but also content search and indexing.

This is the digital curb-cut effect—features created for one group that improve the experience for all.

1.10 Accessibility in the Era of Automation

AI-driven systems introduce new dimensions of complexity. Automated decision-making—like chatbots and personalized interfaces—must themselves be accessible.

Developers must ask:

- Can screen readers interpret dynamically generated responses?
- Do conversational interfaces support keyboard-only users?
- Do speech models understand diverse accents and speech patterns?

AI must not only perform accessible tasks but also be trained to recognize diversity as a core principle. Accessibility is not just what AI does—it is what it understands.

1.11 Emerging AI Applications for Accessibility

AI Applications and Accessibility Impact

Domain	AI Application	Impact
Vision	Automated alt text (Azure, Google Cloud Vision)	Rapid and scalable image description
Hearing	Speech-to-text (Whisper, Otter.ai)	Real-time captioning for meetings and media
Motor	Gesture and eye-tracking	Interaction without physical input devices
Cognitive	Text simplification, summarization	Reduced cognitive load and improved comprehension
Testing	AI-based audits (axe AI, Evinced, Siteimprove)	Detection beyond static rule sets

These innovations mark the transition from accessibility as a manual inspection to a machine-augmented design process.

1.12 The Developer's Role in the AI Accessibility Era

Developers now face a dual challenge:

- Building accessible AI interfaces—ensuring inclusivity in chatbots, recommendation engines, and adaptive layouts.

- Using AI responsibly—avoiding bias and ensuring equitable outcomes.

This requires literacy in both WCAG and AI principles. Developers must know how to evaluate model outputs for fairness and context, expose AI interfaces to assistive technology APIs, and integrate accessibility metrics into CI/CD workflows. Tomorrow's accessibility engineer must think like both a software developer and a data ethicist.

1.13 The Cultural Transformation

Accessibility is no longer "extra work." It is a marker of organizational maturity. Leading companies embed accessibility into every design review and sprint cycle. AI reinforces this by integrating checks into the tools developers already use—for example:

- VS Code extensions highlighting ARIA issues in real time.
- Figma AI plugins simulating low-vision experiences.
- CI/CD pipelines performing continuous accessibility audits.

By shifting accessibility left into design and development phases, organizations dramatically lower cost and increase consistency.

1.14 The Emotional Dimension

Accessibility is often quantified—contrast ratios, audit scores—but its true essence is emotional. A user who feels understood will return; one who feels excluded will leave. AI's greatest promise lies not only in detecting barriers but in creating empathetic interfaces that respond to user behavior. For instance, a voice assistant might slow its speech when sensing hesitation, or a reading interface might switch to audio when detecting fatigue. Here, technology transcends engineering—it becomes empathy in action.

1.15 The Risk of "AI-Washing" Accessibility

Not all "AI accessibility" solutions deliver what they claim. Many overlays promise automatic compliance but often disrupt assistive technologies and mask underlying issues.

True AI accessibility is not about quick fixes—it is about integrating intelligence into design from the ground up. Responsible solutions emphasize transparency and explainability, human override and control, continuous retraining with real user data, and collaboration with disability communities.

1.16 Metrics That Matter

Improvement demands measurement. Standard metrics include:

- Lighthouse accessibility scores (0–100).
- WCAG conformance levels (A, AA, AAA).
- User sentiment from assistive-device interactions.
- Task completion rates across personas.

AI introduces adaptive metrics—learning systems that correlate accessibility enhancements with tangible UX outcomes. Accessibility thus becomes a self-improving, data-informed discipline.

1.17 Accessibility as Innovation

Accessibility has repeatedly proven to drive innovation. VoiceOver, Seeing AI, and Live Caption began as accessibility features but became mainstream advantages. AI continues this pattern: OCR improves document scanning, captioning boosts SEO, and predictive focus management simplifies navigation. Accessibility is not a constraint on innovation—it is its catalyst.

1.18 Developer Takeaways

For Front-End Engineers

- Embed automated accessibility checks (axe-core, Lighthouse CI).
- Validate AI-generated content for relevance and context.
- Ensure all components support ARIA, keyboard, and screen-reader interactions.
- Integrate accessibility telemetry into analytics.

For Accessibility Specialists

- Leverage AI-based auditing tools (Evinced, Siteimprove, Deque).
- Collaborate with ML teams to ensure dataset fairness.
- Treat AI as a collaborator, not an authority.

For Organizations

- Make accessibility continuous, not campaign-based.
- Use AI to amplify empathy, not outsource responsibility.

1.19 Closing Reflection

Accessibility has always been about human ingenuity—designers and engineers finding new ways to include everyone. Artificial intelligence, in all its complexity, is simply the next chapter of that story.

The machines are now learning what humanity has always known: inclusion is not a technical feature—it is a human right. With AI, we finally have the computational power to make that belief scalable.

The chapters that follow explore how models, frameworks, and data can transform this belief into practice—building a world where accessibility is not a compliance task but an intelligent, ongoing conversation between humans and technology.

From WCAG to AI: Evolution of Inclusive Standards

2.1 Origins of Accessibility Standards

The web was conceived as a universal medium, yet its early design excluded many users. In the 1990s, accessibility was managed informally through plain HTML and rudimentary alt attributes. This changed when the World Wide Web Consortium (W3C) launched the Web Accessibility Initiative (WAI) to formalize inclusion.

By 1999, the first Web Content Accessibility Guidelines (WCAG 1.0) were introduced, outlining testable checkpoints for text alternatives, color contrast, and keyboard navigation. These guidelines codified a truth long understood by designers: accessibility could be defined, measured, and implemented.

However, as the web evolved from static pages to dynamic, app-like experiences, the original framework began to falter. WCAG 1.0 was built for documents, not for interactive systems powered by virtual DOMs, single-page applications, or AI-driven layouts. The question was no longer what to display, but how to adapt seamlessly to diverse users.

2.2 WCAG 2.x — From Checklists to Principles

In 2008, WCAG 2.0 redefined accessibility around four enduring principles:

WCAG 2.0 Principles and Examples

Principle	Meaning	Example
Perceivable	Information must be available to all senses.	Provide text alternatives for non-text content.
Operable	Users must be able to interact through multiple input methods.	Ensure all functions are keyboard-accessible.
Understandable	Content and operation must be intuitive and consistent.	Use predictable navigation and behavior.
Robust	Content must be interpretable by assistive technologies.	Use valid semantic HTML and ARIA roles.

These principles were deliberately technology-agnostic, allowing WCAG to remain relevant for years. Yet the framework still relied heavily on human judgment—no automated tool could assess whether content was "understandable" or whether a layout was "predictable." That interpretive gap laid the groundwork for AI integration.

2.3 WCAG 2.1 and 2.2 — Expanding the Scope

With the rise of mobile and touch-based interfaces, WCAG 2.1 (2018) and WCAG 2.2 (2023) extended coverage to low-vision, cognitive, and motor accessibility. Key additions included:

- **1.4.10 Reflow:** Content must reflow properly at up to 400% zoom without loss of information.
- **1.4.13 Content on Hover or Focus:** Pop-ups must be dismissible and persistent.
- **2.5.1 Pointer Gestures:** Actions must be possible using a single pointer without complex gestures.
- **2.5.7 Dragging Movements:** Alternatives to drag-and-drop must be provided.

AI is particularly adept at enforcing these rules. Machine learning can detect layout breakage at high zoom levels, identify focus traps, or flag non-dismissible overlays—areas where conventional linters fail but pattern recognition excels.

2.4 WCAG 3.0 ("Silver") — Shifting Toward Outcomes

The upcoming WCAG 3.0, known as Silver, represents a fundamental paradigm shift. Rather than relying on binary pass/fail tests, it introduces graded outcomes that measure user experience quality.

Instead of asking, "Does this button have a label?" the new approach asks, "Can users reliably identify this button's purpose?" This subtle change enables AI to contribute meaningfully: machine learning models can analyze large-scale interaction data to assess the reliability of user comprehension.

AI Supports WCAG 3.0 by:

- Simulating user testing through assistive technology models.
- Conducting automated contrast and focus analysis.
- Estimating text readability and cognitive load.

Compliance thus evolves from a static benchmark to a context-aware, adaptive measurement of accessibility.

2.5 Assistive Technology Standards and Interoperability

Accessibility does not end with WCAG—it relies on robust interoperability between browsers and assistive technologies. Foundational standards include:

- **ARIA:** Accessible Rich Internet Applications—extends semantic meaning for dynamic interfaces.
- **AT-SPI:** Assistive Technology Service Provider Interface—the Linux accessibility bridge.
- **UI Automation (Windows)** and **AXAPI (macOS):** APIs that expose UI data to assistive tools.

AI strengthens these layers by automatically identifying element roles and relationships. For example, a model can detect that a `<div>` behaves like a button and suggest replacing it with a proper `<button>` element.

Automation must be tempered with human oversight—misapplied roles can create chaos for screen readers. AI assists; humans validate.

2.6 Toolchains Evolving Through AI

Conventional vs AI-Driven Accessibility Tools

Category	Conventional Approach	AI-Driven Evolution
Linters	Static rule enforcement (e.g., eslint-plugin-jsx-a11y)	Predictive linting based on historical defect patterns.
Audits	Deterministic WCAG checks (Lighthouse, axe)	Probabilistic audits estimating user friction and severity.
Design Review	Manual color and font checks	AI simulations of low-vision and color-blind conditions.

For developers, this marks a major shift: tools are no longer static rulebooks but adaptive learning companions.

2.7 Data-Driven Accessibility Metrics

AI's most profound contribution is data. Traditional WCAG testing operates in isolation—criteria are either met or not. AI introduces continuous, evidence-based evaluation through:

- Interaction telemetry: Tracking focus patterns to uncover keyboard bottlenecks.
- Model-based scoring: Weighing issues by probability and severity.
- Adaptive benchmarks: Tailoring accessibility KPIs for distinct user personas (e.g., low-vision or cognitive users).

This integration bridges the gap between technical compliance and actual user experience, establishing feedback loops where accessibility standards evolve with empirical insight.

2.8 The Emerging AI Standards Ecosystem

- **EU AI Act:** Classifies AI by risk, mandating transparency—directly relevant to accessibility tools affecting disabled users.
- **ISO/IEC TR 29138-2:** Defines accessibility metadata for ICT products.
- **W3C Accessible Platform Architectures (APA):** Investigates AI integration within accessibility APIs.

These frameworks reflect a shared recognition: machine judgment must remain accountable to human ethics.

2.9 From Compliance to Continuous Conformance

1. Detection: AI monitors code changes to predict potential violations.
2. Correction: Automated pull request comments suggest WCAG-aligned fixes.
3. Validation: User telemetry verifies whether issues are truly resolved.

This mirrors the DevOps philosophy—accessibility becomes a living, measurable process embedded in the development pipeline.

2.10 Interpreting WCAG at Scale with AI

WCAG's human-readable nature limits automation. Large Language Models (LLMs) are now being trained to translate guidelines into machine logic.

Example:

> Given a React component, identify violations of WCAG 2.1 SC 1.3.1 (Info and Relationships).

An LLM can parse the DOM, understand component intent, and flag missing landmarks—something rule-based tools often overlook. This evolution turns WCAG from a static document into a machine-interpretable API—a standard that learns.

2.11 AI and ARIA — Toward Smarter Semantics

While ARIA enriches web semantics, misuse can easily create confusion. AI helps balance power with precision.

```
<div role="button" aria-pressed="false">Play</div>
```

Better:

```
<button aria-pressed="false">Play</button>
```

AI doesn't just insert markup—it infers intent, ensuring semantics match function. This capability turns ARIA from a potential liability into a tool of clarity.

2.12 Bridging Standards and AI Research

- Transformer models estimating cognitive load from UI designs.
- Vision models simulating low-vision experiences for testing.
- NLP systems generating WCAG-compliant interface copy.

These studies form the foundation of future frameworks—where AI not only enforces standards but helps shape them.

2.13 Ethical Guardrails in AI-Driven Standards

- **Bias:** Models trained on limited datasets risk neglecting non-Western or intersectional disability contexts.
- **Over-simplification:** Automated text simplification can unintentionally patronize users.
- **Opacity:** If AI deems content "accessible," transparency is essential to justify its reasoning.

Future standards must require AI systems to disclose confidence levels, decision criteria, and limitations—ensuring accountability in algorithmic accessibility.

2.14 Accessibility Standards as Living Systems

The age of static rulebooks is ending. Accessibility standards must evolve like software—iteratively and empirically. AI can help maintain this cycle by analyzing millions of audit reports to detect false positives, coverage gaps, and real-world usability data. This represents machine-assisted standardization: faster, more accurate, and globally inclusive.

2.15 Case Study — Automating Contrast Compliance

Color contrast is among WCAG's most measurable requirements, yet one of the most frequently violated. AI-based systems can analyze DOM structures, compute relative luminance, simulate color-blind perception, and predict legibility using deep-learning vision models. They then recommend accessible palettes that meet AA/AAA criteria while preserving brand consistency—transforming contrast checking into perceptual optimization aligned with human vision.

2.16 AI in Policy, Reporting, and Governance

- Natural language summaries mapping violations to specific WCAG criteria.
- Predictive risk scoring based on issue severity and recurrence.
- Continuous monitoring through AI agents that scan live environments.

The result: a transparent, data-driven accessibility posture suitable for large organizations navigating multiple frameworks (WCAG, ADA, Section 508).

2.17 Developer Takeaways

1. Recognize evolution: WCAG is shifting toward adaptive, AI-informed interpretation.
2. Adopt AI responsibly: Automate detection, but retain human review.

3. Integrate early: Embed audits into CI/CD; train AI on your design system.
4. Contribute feedback: Share data and edge cases with standards bodies.
5. Ensure transparency: If AI certifies accessibility, publish its confidence levels and rationale.

2.18 The Broader Vision

Accessibility standards began as a means to codify fairness; AI offers a way to scale it. The challenge lies in preserving meaning amid automation. The goal is not an algorithm that ticks every WCAG box, but a web that adapts fluidly to human diversity. Standards will remain the foundation, but AI will form the scaffolding—supporting, learning, and evolving with our collective understanding of inclusion.

Understanding Digital Barriers

3.1 The Invisible Walls of the Web

Every inaccessible website is built with good intentions—and invisible barriers. Developers often remain unaware of these obstacles because their own senses and devices mask them. Yet for millions of users, such barriers are as tangible as locked doors.

A digital barrier is any technical or design decision that prevents, delays, or confuses user interaction—particularly for individuals with disabilities. Some barriers are overt, such as unlabeled buttons or missing captions. Others are more insidious: inconsistent heading structures, unannounced context changes, or icons distinguished solely by color.

Artificial intelligence cannot remove what humans refuse to acknowledge. Its first contribution, therefore, is visibility—the ability to detect, quantify, and explain barriers at scale. AI transforms accessibility from sporadic inspection into a measurable, systematic discipline.

3.2 The Four Categories of Barriers

Accessibility professionals commonly classify barriers according to four primary domains of disability. Each presents distinctive challenges—and unique opportunities for AI-driven solutions.

Barrier Domains and AI Opportunities

Domain	Common Barriers	AI Opportunities
Visual	Low contrast, missing alt text, reflow failures	Computer vision models for contrast measurement and context-aware image description
Auditory	Absent captions or transcripts	Speech-to-text and language models generating synchronized captions
Motor	Small targets, drag-only gestures, timeouts	Behavioral AI detecting interaction friction and recommending alternative patterns
Cognitive	Complex language, inconsistent navigation	NLP systems simplifying text and optimizing information hierarchy

By aligning AI analysis with these domains, developers can focus investment and engineering effort where it will have the most meaningful impact.

3.3 Visual Barriers and Computer Vision

Contrast and Color Dependence

Poor contrast remains one of the most frequent WCAG violations (SC 1.4.3, 1.4.11). Conventional linters provide ratio-based results but ignore context. AI-based vision models simulate human perception, testing color palettes under low-vision and color-blindness conditions. Rather than outputting a simple "fails AA contrast," they recommend palette adjustments that preserve brand integrity while meeting luminance requirements.

Images Without Meaningful Alt Text

While missing `alt` attributes are easily detected, missing meaning is not. Modern captioning models, trained on extensive datasets, can propose candidate descriptions. Yet human review remains essential—AI may produce a technically correct but semantically shallow caption ("person running") where true context matters ("blind athlete finishing a marathon"). Empathy cannot be automated.

Layout and Zoom Behavior

When users zoom to 400%, text reflow issues frequently break layouts. AI-powered visual regression testing—essentially a neural "spot-the-difference" approach—can detect overlapping elements and clipped content. When combined with CSS grid heuristics, these systems identify problem breakpoints and notify developers automatically.

3.4 Auditory Barriers and Speech AI

Captions and Transcripts

WCAG's 1.2 success criteria mandate captions for both prerecorded and live media. AI-driven speech recognition engines can achieve high accuracy on clear audio and be fine-tuned for domain-specific vocabulary. However, human editing remains critical for speaker attribution, punctuation, and emotional nuance—areas where AI lacks sensitivity.

Sound Cues and Auditory Overload

Some interfaces rely exclusively on audio feedback. AI auditing tools can parse source code to identify event-based sound triggers and verify whether corresponding visual cues exist. Conversely, AI-assisted acoustic profilers evaluate sound frequency and volume, helping designers accommodate hearing-aid users and prevent sensory fatigue.

3.5 Motor Barriers and Predictive Interaction

Motor impairments affect fine motor control, coordination, and steadiness. Common barriers include:

- Small interactive targets (below WCAG 2.5.5's 44×44 px minimum)
- Drag-only actions without keyboard equivalents
- Session timeouts too short for slower users

AI's Role

Machine learning models can analyze pointer trajectories to detect hesitation or repeated errors—signs of difficulty. Aggregated ethically and anonymized, such data supports adaptive UIs: automatically enlarging buttons, extending timeouts, or enabling gesture alternatives.

To preserve privacy, these models often run locally using frameworks such as TensorFlow.js or WebNN, enabling real-time, device-side inference.

3.6 Cognitive and Neurological Barriers

Cognitive accessibility is the least automated and the most human. Challenges include complex copy, inconsistent navigation, and processes requiring heavy memory load.

Natural Language Processing (NLP) supports cognitive accessibility by:

- Measuring reading level and recommending simplifications.
- Detecting ambiguous or passive phrasing.
- Generating simplified summaries while preserving meaning.

Example:

"Customers utilizing our omnichannel fulfilment interface may experience intermittent latency." becomes "You may notice short delays when checking out online."

Such rewriting retains intent but reduces cognitive load—directly aligning with WCAG 3.0's Understandable principle.

3.7 Temporal and Environmental Constraints

Not all barriers stem from permanent disabilities. Situational constraints—sun glare, noise, or poor connectivity—can temporarily disable anyone. AI systems can adapt dynamically: detecting ambient noise, device brightness, or network speed and switching modes accordingly (e.g., from video to transcript, or from animation to static layout). This represents situational accessibility—inclusion that adapts in real time.

3.8 Compound Barriers in Modern Interfaces

Single-page applications often combine multiple accessibility challenges: a modal triggered by voice command may open off-screen, trap focus, and lack description. AI-enhanced crawlers emulate "synthetic users" via headless browsers and screen-reader emulators, detecting lost focus and unannounced DOM changes invisible to static validators.

3.9 From Detection to Interpretation

Detection alone is insufficient. AI may flag "generic link text" but cannot infer why a designer wrote "Learn more." Emerging research blends detection with intent inference, analyzing context to determine whether repeated links lead to identical destinations. The model then suggests consolidation, evolving from compliance enforcement to design reasoning.

3.10 User Modeling and Personalization

Accessibility is inherently personal. Two users with the same visual condition may prefer different contrast or typography. AI enables adaptive profiles that learn preferences from behavior—offering permanent zoom or color settings without explicit toggles.

Privacy remains paramount: preferences should be stored locally, ensuring compliance with GDPR and the EU AI Act.

3.11 Testing with Synthetic Users

Traditional QA depends on scarce assistive technology testers. AI enables synthetic agents that simulate screen-reader, keyboard-only, or voice-based interactions. These agents can crawl DOMs, identify focus traps, and record accessibility telemetry.

Note: Simulations do not replace real users—they expand coverage and catch regressions early.

3.12 Quantifying Accessibility Debt

Accessibility debt parallels technical debt: the backlog of unresolved accessibility issues. AI analytics can quantify it by:

- Assigning severity weights based on WCAG criteria.
- Estimating remediation effort using historical fix data.
- Tracking progress through dashboards and trendlines.

This reframes accessibility as a measurable engineering discipline, driving accountability and executive visibility.

3.13 The Human Factor: Context and Culture

AI can map structure, but not experience. Cultural context defines what "accessible" feels like—language direction, idioms, tone, and color symbolism differ globally. Therefore, accessibility models must be trained and validated across languages and regions. True inclusion begins when AI systems themselves are designed inclusively.

3.14 Case Study — Detecting Keyboard Traps

A global e-commerce platform implemented AI-driven audits across millions of product pages. The model identified keyboard traps by analyzing user telemetry—flagging instances where more than 15 consecutive Tab presses failed to advance focus.

Automated screenshots and DOM snapshots were attached to issue tickets, cutting issue resolution time by 70%. AI didn't make the site accessible—it made inaccessibility visible.

3.15 Ethical Boundaries in Barrier Detection

Collecting behavioral data raises ethical concerns. Responsible implementation requires:

- Aggregation at the population, not individual, level.
- Obfuscation of identifiers.
- Clear consent mechanisms and opt-outs.

Accessibility must empower, not surveil. AI's role is to sense friction, not infer identity.

3.16 Developer Checklist — Eliminating Barriers

Visual

- Ensure color contrast $\geq$ 4.5:1 (AA) or 7:1 (AAA).
- Provide accurate alt text; review AI-generated captions manually.
- Validate layout reflow at 400% zoom.

Auditory

- Caption all media; offer transcripts.
- Provide visual equivalents for sound cues.

Motor

- Guarantee keyboard operability.
- Maintain adequate target size and spacing.
- Review gesture and timeout logic.

Cognitive

- Use plain language and predictable navigation.
- Avoid abrupt context changes.

Embedding AI auditing at each step transforms this checklist from static guidance into a live feedback system.

3.17 Developer Takeaways

- Visibility precedes remedy—AI exposes barriers at scale.
- Human insight remains indispensable—context and empathy cannot be automated.
- Accessibility data drives adoption—quantified debt influences business priorities.
- Edge AI protects privacy—client-side intelligence enables personalization safely.

3.18 Closing Thoughts

Understanding digital barriers forms the foundation of AI-driven accessibility. Empathy cannot be automated—but awareness can. Each inaccessible interface reflects an assumption: that everyone perceives, hears, and interacts as the developer does. AI challenges those assumptions systematically, transforming awareness into action.

The next chapter explores how design and development teams operationalize this knowledge through intelligent tooling—making accessibility continuous, measurable, and self-sustaining.

The Rise of AI-Driven Accessibility Tools

4.1 Why Automation Became Essential

For years, accessibility relied on human diligence—manual audits, fixes, and checklists. As digital ecosystems expanded to thousands of dynamic pages, that model became unsustainable. No QA team can manually retest every iteration. AI-driven accessibility emerged to close this scalability gap—transforming accessibility from an occasional audit into a continuous, adaptive process.

4.2 Defining AI-Driven Accessibility

AI-driven accessibility applies machine learning, natural language processing, and computer vision to detect, explain, and remediate accessibility issues throughout the development lifecycle.

Lifecycle Stages: Traditional vs AI-Augmented

Stage	Traditional Approach	AI-Augmented Method
Design	Manual color and typography checks	Vision models simulate low-vision perception and suggest compliant palettes

Stage	Traditional Approach	AI-Augmented Method
Development	Rule-based linters (e.g., eslint-plugin-jsx-a11y)	Predictive linting based on code patterns and historical defect data
Testing	Static QA audits	Synthetic users navigate apps using reinforcement learning
Content	Manually written alt text	AI-generated captions and transcripts with human review
Monitoring	Scheduled Lighthouse scans	Continuous telemetry and anomaly detection

AI doesn't replace WCAG—it operationalizes it.

4.3 The Architectural Shift in Accessibility Tooling

Modern accessibility stacks typically include three intelligent layers:

1. **Detection Layer** — Identifies probable barriers.
2. **Interpretation Layer** — Assesses impact and confidence.
3. **Action Layer** — Suggests or applies fixes while feeding results back to training models.

Accessibility tools now behave like autonomous QA agents, learning from developer behavior and improving with every release.

4.4 AI-Powered Tool Landscape

Categories of AI-Powered Accessibility Tools

Category	Description	Example Tools
Audit Engines	ML-enhanced automated scanning	axe AI; Evinced; Siteimprove Intelligence
Design Assistants	Figma plugins simulating vision conditions	Stark AI; Contrastive
IDE Extensions	Real-time accessibility hints	GitHub Copilot Accessibility Mode; Deque VS Extension
Browser Agents	Live usage monitoring and recommendations	Microsoft Clarity AI; UserWay Monitor
Content Analyzers	NLP tools assessing tone and readability	Hemingway AI; Grammarly Accessibility Mode

Developer Tip: Choose tools that learn from your own codebase. Contextual learning minimizes false positives and maximizes relevance.

4.5 Continuous Auditing at Scale

A global retailer integrated AI auditing into its CI/CD pipeline. Each pull request triggered automated accessibility tests across 200+ templates. The system compared diffs with historical issues and flagged likely regressions (e.g., "Contrast issue — 84% confidence"). Inline comments linked directly to WCAG references. Result: accessibility defects decreased by 63% over three sprints. Humans validated edge cases, but AI handled the scale.

4.6 How Machine Learning Improves Accuracy

- **Supervised learning** identifies patterns in labeled accessibility examples.
- **Unsupervised clustering** reveals new anti-patterns.
- **Reinforcement learning** adjusts confidence weights based on developer feedback.

Over time, these feedback loops produce adaptive tools that align with organizational behavior and design systems.

4.7 Accessibility as Telemetry

Accessibility metrics are no longer static reports—they are live data streams. Dashboards now track trendlines for color contrast, keyboard navigation, and ARIA accuracy. Anomaly detection highlights regressions post-deployment, much like performance monitoring.

Developer Tip: Treat accessibility metrics as first-class telemetry. Observe, visualize, and respond continuously.

4.8 Generative AI for Learning and Documentation

Conversational AI assistants trained on WCAG and ARIA standards can provide real-time guidance:

- Why does role="presentation" conflict with tabindex?
- Suggest a fix for WCAG 2.1 SC 1.4.13.

These systems democratize expertise—making accessibility literacy accessible to every developer.

4.9 Predictive Testing and Risk Scoring

By analyzing historical bug data, AI models can predict which components are most likely to fail accessibility standards. This enables teams to prioritize testing for high-risk areas—such as modals, custom sliders, and third-party widgets—before issues reach production.

4.10 Computer Vision in Audit Pipelines

Computer vision extends beyond alt text. It verifies spatial alignment, padding consistency, and focus visibility—simulating how low-vision users perceive layouts. (See Chapter 6 for deeper coverage of perceptual models.)

4.11 Integrating Accessibility into CI/CD

1. **Pre-Commit:** IDE plugin validates ARIA roles.
2. **Build Stage:** AI scanners assess compiled code.
3. **Pre-Production:** Synthetic users emulate assistive tech.
4. **Post-Deploy:** Live telemetry gathers user feedback.
5. **Model Update:** Data continuously retrains detection accuracy.

Accessibility thus becomes part of DevOps discipline—a living, measurable practice.

4.12 Limitations and False Confidence

- **Context ignorance:** Models can't interpret humor or cultural nuance.
- **Bias:** Training data may reflect Western design conventions.
- **Overlays:** Many "auto-compliance" scripts degrade user experience.

Automation must augment human expertise, not replace it.

4.13 Ethical and Legal Implications

As AI audits accessibility, transparency becomes a legal and ethical requirement. Organizations should:

- Disclose AI usage in reports.
- Retain human accountability for final approval.
- Log AI confidence scores and reasoning—crucial under the EU AI Act.

Developer Tip: "AI-assisted" does not mean "AI-certified." Always include human review.

4.14 Accessibility Bots and Conversational Assistants

Some design tools now feature embedded AI chatbots capable of contextual dialogue:

- "Is this font legible on dark backgrounds?"
- "Add focus outlines to all interactive elements."

These assistants transform accessibility from a specialist task to a collaborative design conversation.

4.15 Case Study — AI in Government CMS

A multilingual government CMS integrated an AI plugin that generated alt text, validated color contrast, and simplified headlines. Confidence scores determined whether content required human review. Within six months, accessibility-related rejections dropped by 58%. AI became a guardian of quality, not a gatekeeper.

4.16 Toward Self-Healing Interfaces

Experimental "self-healing" interfaces are emerging. They detect and automatically correct common accessibility failures:

- Repairing focus order dynamically.
- Adjusting color contrast in real time.
- Generating placeholder alt text until human review.

While still research-stage, these systems represent the next frontier of autonomous accessibility maintenance.

4.17 Summary and Developer Takeaways

Core Insights

- AI shifts accessibility from reactive fixes to proactive prevention.
- Continuous feedback turns compliance into a living process.
- Integration with IDEs and CI/CD embeds accessibility in everyday workflows.
- Human validation and ethical transparency remain essential.

Action Steps

- Integrate AI audits early in development.
- Treat accessibility metrics as telemetry.
- Avoid "overlay" quick fixes.
- Stay current with WCAG 3.0 and AI policy evolution.

4.18 Looking Ahead

The following chapters explore the specialized intelligences driving this transformation—how language models simplify content (Chapter 5), computer vision interprets images (Chapter 6), and voice interfaces enable multimodal accessibility (Chapter 7). Together, these advances reveal a powerful truth: AI doesn't merely check accessibility—it helps create it.

Natural Language Processing for Comprehension

5.1 Why Language Matters to Accessibility

The majority of digital barriers are not visual—they're linguistic. Complex copy, inconsistent tone, and unexplained jargon can exclude users as effectively as a missing `alt` attribute. For neurodiverse audiences, non-native speakers, and readers with cognitive disabilities, language is the primary interface. Natural Language Processing (NLP) offers developers a way to measure and adapt written content intelligently. Where accessibility once focused on markup, NLP turns attention to meaning.

5.2 From Text Validation to Text Intelligence

Traditional readability tools (for example, Flesch-Kincaid) quantify syllables and sentence length. They're useful but crude: a sentence can be short yet confusing ("Tap the toggle to disable active state"). AI-driven NLP goes further by understanding context and intent. It evaluates what is being said, to whom, and why.

Capabilities: Classic Tools vs NLP Enhancements

Capability	Classic Tool	NLP Enhancement
Readability	Average word/sentence length	Understands domain context and target audience
Terminology	Dictionary look-ups	Identifies brand or technical jargon automatically
Tone	Not measured	Analyses sentiment and formality
Structure	Word count only	Detects logical flow and cohesion between sentences

5.3 Accessibility and Cognitive Load

WCAG 2.2 Success Criterion 3.1 requires "readable and under-standable content." Yet compliance is not clarity. Cognitive load—the mental effort required to process information—is the true barrier.

AI models can estimate this by tracking:

- Average sentence complexity.
- Density of abstract terms.
- Use of negation and conditional clauses.
- Consistency of terminology across pages.

The result is a Comprehension Score, not just a readability grade.

Real-World Example

A financial services portal used an NLP engine to rewrite form instructions. Comprehension errors (measured by incomplete submissions) dropped by 37%. The engine flagged sentences containing more than one conditional verb as high risk.

5.4 Simplification without Dilution

A common fear is that simplification "dumbs down" content. Effective NLP systems perform semantic compression—retaining meaning while reducing linguistic noise.

Example transformation

```
Before - "Applicants who intend to utilize

After  - "You need to fill in the registra
```

5.5 Multilingual and Cross-Cultural Understanding

Global products often translate content literally, not functionally. NLP models trained on multilingual corpora adapt tone and idiom per locale. They can detect when translation creates cognitive conflict.

Developer Takeaway: Use AI translation with post-editing guidelines. Automated output should be reviewed for cultural appropriateness, not just grammar.

5.6 Semantic Labelling and ARIA Integration

NLP can bridge content and structure by automatically suggesting ARIA labels. For instance, when detecting a pattern like "Add to Basket," it can recommend:

```
<button aria-label="Add item to shopping basket">Add
```

This ensures that labels mirror visible text and intent, preventing screen-reader ambiguity.

5.7 AI Copy Assistants in Design Workflows

Modern design tools use language models to evaluate content directly within layouts. They analyze font size versus reading level and flag copy that is too dense for mobile viewports. Designers receive plain-language suggestions such as: "Consider shorter instruction text—reading level estimated at CEFR C1 (advanced)." Embedding NLP at design time avoids expensive late-stage rewrites.

5.8 Detecting Ambiguity and Inconsistency

Ambiguity is a hidden accessibility risk. Words like "next," "submit," or "continue" can be interpreted differently depending on context. NLP models trained on task-flow data can flag ambiguous phrases by checking for multiple possible actions following the same label.

Developers then receive a prompt: "Clarify button purpose—multiple 'next' actions detected."

5.9 Automatic Summarization and Personalized Content

For long policy documents or tutorials, summarization models can produce short versions targeted to reading goals:

- **Overview Mode:** three-sentence summary for quick scan.
- **Detailed Mode:** paragraph-by-paragraph breakdown.
- **Assistive Mode:** simple-language version aligned with WCAG 3.0 Understandable criteria.

Personalization engines combine these outputs with user profiles (language proficiency, preferred reading speed) to deliver customized experiences without manual authoring.

5.10 Voice and Text Synergy

NLP is the bridge between spoken and written interaction. When paired with Automatic Speech Recognition (ASR) and Text-to-Speech (TTS), it enables dynamic translation between modalities:

- Voice input → NLP parses intent → semantic action in UI.
- Screen-reader output → NLP simplifies phrasing before speech synthesis.

Chapter 7 expands on voice interfaces and multimodal accessibility.

5.11 NLP for Error Prevention and Form Validation

Complex forms are a common source of abandonment. NLP models can interpret error messages for clarity and tone, rewriting technical feedback into helpful guidance.

```
Before: "Input invalid per regex constraint."
After:  "Please enter a valid email address (e.g., a
```

They can also detect when multiple fields ask for similar information and recommend consolidation for cognitive efficiency.

5.12 Accessibility Chatbots and Guided Assistance

NLP-based chatbots serve as assistive layers for users who struggle with navigation or language. Instead of browsing menus, users can ask plainly: "Show me how to reset my password." The bot parses intent, executes actions, and responds in text or speech.

- Bots should announce their presence to screen readers.
- Conversation state must be keyboard accessible.
- NLP models should handle spelling errors and non-standard grammar.

5.13 Bias and Fairness in Language Models

AI mirrors its training data. If that data contains ableist, gendered, or cultural biases, models can generate harmful language.

- Run outputs through toxicity filters and bias detectors.
- Use datasets curated by diverse linguistic communities.
- Document model limitations in a model card or datasheet.

Developer Takeaway: Fair language is accessible language. Bias mitigation is part of a developer's accessibility responsibility.

5.14 Integrating NLP into Development Pipelines

Practical workflow example:

1. **Pre-commit:** Run a text-lint check for readability and terminology.
2. **Build stage:** NLP engine generates and evaluates `alt` text and error messages.
3. **Review:** Accessibility bot comments on pull requests with clarity suggestions.
4. **Deploy:** Telemetry collects user interactions (for example, error retry rates) to retrain language models.

The result is a continuous language-quality loop similar to DevOps for code.

5.15 Real-World Example – Simplifying Government Communication

The U.K. Government Digital Service experimented with AI simplification tools to rewrite legacy content on GOV.UK. Models scanned over one million pages and highlighted complex phrases (> CEFR C1). Human editors approved roughly 45% of AI suggestions directly; the rest informed style-guide updates. Outcome: average reading level dropped from 14 to 10 years of education without loss of accuracy.

5.16 The Next Frontier – Emotion and Empathy

Emerging research focuses on affective NLP—models that sense user emotion from language signals. For accessibility, this could mean:

- Detecting frustration in chat inputs and triggering simpler responses.
- Adapting tone for anxious users during onboarding.
- Providing empathetic feedback ("I see that didn't work—let's try another way").

When applied ethically, emotional AI can make interfaces feel more supportive and human-centred.

5.17 Limitations of NLP in Accessibility

- Context misjudgment: AI may simplify legal or medical content too aggressively.
- Language coverage: Minority languages are often under-represented.
- Privacy: Processing user text requires GDPR-compliant data handling.
- Latency: Large models can slow real-time interfaces; edge inference helps.

Always include manual review and fallback mechanisms.

5.18 Developer Checklist

- Use AI readability checkers during content reviews.
- Validate `alt` text and error messages with NLP for clarity.
- Add multilingual support via context-aware translation.
- Audit models for bias and maintain human oversight.
- Keep logs of AI recommendations and editor actions for traceability.

5.19 Closing Reflection

Language is where accessibility meets emotion. A clean semantic DOM is useless if the copy confuses or intimidates. NLP gives developers a way to measure comprehension objectively and optimize it continuously. The goal isn't to replace writers—it's to empower them to communicate clearly to every reader, regardless of ability or background. As AI matures, we move from static WCAG rules toward living language systems that adapt tone, complexity, and delivery to the user in real time. In doing so, we bridge the final gap between what we say and how people understand it.

Computer Vision for Visual Accessibility

6.1 Seeing Through Machines

Human sight interprets colour, depth, and context effortlessly. For users with visual impairments, software must fill that gap. Computer Vision (CV) — the branch of AI that teaches machines to "see" — has become a crucial accessibility enabler, converting pixels into meaning. From image description and text recognition to colour-contrast auditing and spatial analysis, CV allows web systems to perceive the interface they present.

6.2 From Pixels to Perception

Classic web accessibility tools view pages as code: DOM nodes and CSS values. Computer-vision tools, by contrast, render pages as visual artefacts and analyze them like a human would.

Comparison of Traditional vs Vision-Based Methods

Capability	Traditional Method	Vision Method
Alt-text checks	Validate the presence of alt attributes	Generate contextual image descriptions via caption models

Capability	Traditional Method	Vision Method
Contrast testing	Compute colour ratios from CSS	Measure luminance from actual rendered pixels
Layout analysis	Parse DOM structure	Segment visual regions to detect clipping or overlap
Text visibility	Check font size	OCR to verify on-screen readability and blur resistance

By treating the interface as an image, AI exposes accessibility defects invisible to static code audits.

6.3 Automatic Alt Text Generation

WCAG 2.1 SC 1.1.1 requires "text alternatives for non-text content." CV models such as CLIP, BLIP-2, and Azure Vision API can produce alt text instantly.

Example Flow

1. Extract image features via convolutional network.
2. Feed embedding into language model.
3. Generate caption: "Person wearing red jacket running on beach."

Developer Guidelines ◈

- Use AI captions as starting points, not final outputs.
- Review for accuracy and relevance ("man" vs "athlete," "dog" vs "guide dog").

- Expose model confidence scores to editors.

Real-World Example ◈

Facebook's "Automatic Alt Text" uses object detection to describe photos for screen-reader users. The system generates structured phrases such as "May contain: two people, outdoor, smiling." It reduced blank image announcements by over 90 %.

6.4 Describing Complex Images

Charts, infographics, and maps pose unique challenges. CV combined with Optical Character Recognition (OCR) can extract labels and axes, while NLP summarizes trends such as: "Bar chart showing quarterly sales increasing from Q1 to Q4, peaking at £2 million." Developers should integrate these AI-generated summaries into `<figure>` or `<table>` captions so assistive technologies announce data meaningfully.

6.5 Colour and Contrast Analysis

Low contrast is among the most frequent WCAG failures. Traditional formulae (`(L1 + 0.05)/(L2 + 0.05) ≥ 4.5:1`) ignore ambient conditions. CV tools simulate vision deficiencies (protanopia, deuteranopia, tritanopia) and real-world lighting to predict legibility as humans perceive it.

Developer Takeaway ◈

Automate contrast audits at build time using rendered screenshots, not CSS tokens. Pixel-level analysis reflects true visual experience.

6.6 Layout and Focus Integrity

Single-page apps often break focus order when elements shift. CV models detect visual movement and highlight when focus indicators disappear or overlap with backgrounds. Paired with DOM analysis, this enables "focus map" visualizations showing how a keyboard user's attention travels across the page.

6.7 Text Detection and OCR for Dynamic Media

AI OCR tools like Tesseract and Google Vision API extract text from images or videos for screen-reader output. When applied to marketing banners or social graphics, they prevent information loss for blind users. Developers can pipe OCR output into ARIA labels or metadata, ensuring machine-readable equivalence.

6.8 Image Quality and Compression Awareness

Blurry or compressed images disproportionately impact low-vision users. Vision models calculate sharpness metrics (SSIM, PSNR) and flag assets below thresholds. This helps CDNs serve adaptive resolutions based on user zoom level and device capability.

6.9 Spatial Navigation and 3-D Contexts

With WebGL and WebXR entering mainstream use, 3-D interfaces pose new barriers. CV pipelines map depth and object boundaries to produce narrative descriptions such as "Object two metres ahead on left." These spatial annotations support haptic or audio feedback for blind gamers and AR users.

6.10 Synthetic Vision Testing

Testing for visual accessibility traditionally involved manual screen-reader runs. AI now generates synthetic vision profiles — simulations of how users with specific impairments perceive the page.

Simulation Types and Examples

Simulation Type	Purpose	Tool Examples
Colour-blindness filters	Verify colour distinguishability	Stark, Polypane, Contrastive AI
Low-vision blur models	Test font legibility and spacing	aXe Vision, Google Accessibility Scanner
Peripheral-vision masking	Assess content layout prioritization	Custom TensorFlow.js simulations

Such visual regressions can be automated within CI/CD to flag contrast drops or misaligned elements after a theme update.

6.11 Real-World Example – Retail Imagery Audit

A large e-commerce brand used a vision model to scan 120 000 product images. It detected lighting inconsistencies that obscured fabric texture for low-vision users and flagged colour families that collapsed under deuteranopia simulation. Post-correction, return rates for colour-sensitive items fell by 12 %.

6.12 AI and AR – Assistive Environments

Mobile apps combine camera feeds and CV to guide navigation. Examples include Microsoft's Seeing AI and Google's Lookout, which describe surroundings and read text aloud. Web technologies (via WebRTC and Web Speech API) can replicate this in progressive web apps, allowing browser-based object recognition for users who decline native installs.

6.13 Model Training and Bias

CV models inherit bias from datasets. If trained mostly on Western imagery, they may mislabel diverse cultures and assistive devices (for example, calling a white cane a "stick").

Mitigation Strategies

- Curate inclusive datasets with global representation.
- Perform error analysis by demographics.
- Expose model limitations in documentation.

Developer Takeaway ◈

AI must see the world accurately before it can describe it accessibly.

6.14 Integrating Vision Checks into Workflow

1. Design phase – Run contrast simulation plugins.
2. Build – Generate and validate AI alt text.

3. QA – Compare rendered screenshots against accessibility base-lines.
4. Post-deploy – Telemetry agent monitors user zoom/contrast preferences to tune future themes.

Vision AI thus forms a feedback loop between design and experience.

6.15 Edge Processing and Privacy

Running CV in the browser (using TensorFlow.js or ONNX Runtime Web) avoids sending images to cloud APIs, preserving privacy and reducing latency. This approach is vital for sensitive contexts such as health records or education.

6.16 Evaluating Model Performance

- **Mean Average Precision (mAP):** object-detection accuracy.
- **BLEU / CIDEr:** caption quality scores.
- **Human evaluation:** crowd-sourced clarity ratings.

Combine quantitative and qualitative feedback for realistic assessment.

6.17 Limitations and Risks

- Over-generation: Verbose captions can overwhelm screen-reader users.
- Context blindness: AI describes objects, not significance.
- Performance: Client-side inference adds CPU load on low-end devices.

- Regulation: Upcoming EU AI Act requires disclosure when AI creates content.

Mitigate by setting confidence thresholds and maintaining human review.

6.18 Developer Checklist

- Integrate AI contrast and layout analysis in build pipeline.
- Use vision APIs for alt-text generation but review outputs.
- Simulate vision impairments during design review.
- Ensure datasets and models are inclusive and documented.
- Prefer edge inference for privacy-critical applications.

6.19 Closing Reflection

Computer Vision has elevated accessibility from syntax to semantics — from code that works to interfaces that see. When used ethically, it extends human sight rather than replacing it, helping developers build webs that describe themselves clearly to everyone. The next chapter completes this trio of senses by exploring Voice Interfaces and Conversational UX — how AI speech technologies make interaction audible, adaptive, and inclusive.

Voice Interfaces and Conversational UX

7.1 From Typing to Talking

The graphical user interface gave the web its visual language; the voice interface gives it a human one. Speaking to computers is no longer science fiction—it is routine through Siri, Alexa, and Google Assistant. For accessibility, voice is transformative: it removes dependence on sight, fine motor control, and even literacy.

Voice interfaces combine three AI pillars:

1. **Automatic Speech Recognition (ASR)** — turns speech into text.
2. **Natural Language Processing (NLP)** — interprets intent and context.
3. **Text-to-Speech (TTS)** — renders spoken output.

Together, they allow the web to listen and speak.

7.2 The Accessibility Promise of Voice

Voice interaction supports a wide spectrum of users:

- **Blind or low-vision users** — navigate without visual cues.
- **Motor impairments** — replace mouse or keyboard input.

- **Cognitive differences** — converse naturally instead of decoding complex UI flows.
- **Situational constraints** — hands-free control while driving or cooking.

As WCAG 3.0 shifts toward outcome-based measures, voice accessibility aligns perfectly: success is judged by whether a user can complete a task, not by how they did it.

7.3 Speech Recognition and Accuracy

Early ASR struggled with accent, dialect, and background noise. Modern neural models (for example, Whisper, Conformer, Deep-Speech 2) can achieve > 95% accuracy in clean audio. The remaining challenge is robustness—understanding diverse voices.

Key techniques

- **Acoustic adaptation** — models fine-tuned on local accents.
- **Noise robustness** — spectral augmentation during training.
- **Punctuation prediction** — adds prosodic cues for readability.

Developer Takeaway: Evaluate ASR systems on real customer data—accents, domain terminology, background noise—not demo clips.

7.4 Command and Control Interfaces

For developers, the simplest voice accessibility win is command mapping: linking verbal phrases to DOM actions.

```
if (voiceCommand.includes("add to basket")) {
  document.querySelector("#addToCart").click();
}
```

Frameworks such as Web Speech API, Alan AI, and Spokestack allow voice triggers without proprietary SDKs. Ensure every spoken command also has a visible counterpart to maintain parity for users who cannot or prefer not to speak.

7.5 Conversational UX — Beyond Commands

Voice becomes truly accessible when it moves from commands to conversations. Conversational UX (CUX) applies dialogue design to tasks—users express goals, not steps.

Example: "Book my next Pilates class at 7 a.m. tomorrow."

AI orchestrates: intent → entities → API call → spoken confirmation. Accessibility benefit: fewer clicks, less memory load, and a natural flow matching human cognition.

7.6 Integrating Voice with Screen Readers

Best practice

- Use ARIA live regions to announce responses (`aria-live="polite"`).
- Keep speech output concise (< 20 seconds).
- Provide textual transcripts for deaf-blind users using refreshable Braille.
- Expose speech controls (pause, replay, speed) via keyboard.

7.7 Real-World Example — Voice Navigation on E-commerce

A sports-apparel brand implemented a Web Speech-based "Voice Shop" mode. Users could say: "Show me men's running shorts in black." The system parsed product category + colour + gender and updated the grid. Testing with blind users showed a 48% faster journey to checkout. Because all voice commands mapped to standard URL parameters, SEO and analytics remained intact.

7.8 Natural Language Understanding for Error Tolerance

Users rarely speak like machines. "Find leggings small size navy" is not the same as "Search for leggings, size S, colour navy." Intent-classification models using BERT or GPT embeddings recognise variants and filler words, reducing friction.

Developer Tip: Store transcripts anonymously; retrain models on mis-recognized phrases to improve inclusivity continuously.

7.9 Multimodal Accessibility

True inclusion blends modalities: voice, touch, vision. A user may begin a process by voice ("open size guide") and finish by tapping. Web Speech API combined with Pointer Events enables such hybrid flows. Ensure consistent focus handling so assistive tech can follow context switches seamlessly.

7.10 Speech Output and Text-to-Speech (TTS)

Synthetic voices have advanced from robotic to expressive. Neural TTS systems (for example, Tacotron 2, VITS) capture intonation and pacing, crucial for comprehension.

Checklist for Inclusive Speech Output

- Offer multiple voice options and speeds.
- Announce state changes succinctly ("Item added to basket").
- Avoid auto-speech without user consent (WCAG 2.2 SC 1.4.2).
- Cache audio locally for performance on low bandwidth.

7.11 Conversational Pattern Design

Developers should think like dialogue architects:

1. **Greeting** — "Hi, how can I help you?"
2. **Intent confirmation** — "Did you mean the black pair in size M?"
3. **Fallbacks** — "Sorry, I did not catch that. You can say 'repeat'."
4. **Exit strategy** — "Done. Would you like to continue shopping?"

Each step maps to a state machine, ensuring predictable behavior and graceful recovery.

7.12 Voice Accessibility and Cognitive Load

For users with memory or processing differences, voice systems can reduce complexity—provided they manage context. AI should summarize choices ("Three options: Classic, Lite, Pro") instead of reading exhaustive lists. Conversational memory models track prior turns, allowing progressive disclosure rather than repetition.

7.13 Handling Silence and Error States

A silent interface can be alarming for blind users. Always respond verbally to errors ("No results found for 'blue mat'"). Implement time-outs gracefully: after 5 seconds of silence, prompt politely ("Still there? You can say 'help'.").

7.14 Voice Analytics and Feedback

Telemetry can measure success rates, misunderstood commands, and latency. Aggregated data helps retrain models and prioritize fixes. Keep recordings anonymized and encrypted; disclose analytics use in privacy statements to maintain trust.

7.15 Cross-Language and Code-Switching

Multilingual users mix languages mid-sentence. Modern ASR models handle code-switching, dynamically detecting language boundaries. For accessibility, this eliminates the need to pre-set language preferences—critical for bilingual regions.

7.16 Ethical Concerns and Privacy

Voice data is personal biometric information. Comply with GDPR and AI Act provisions:

• Obtain explicit consent before recording.

- Store voice embeddings, not raw audio, where possible.
- Allow local (on-device) processing for sensitive contexts.
- Provide delete-my-data endpoints.

Voice accessibility must never come at the cost of user autonomy.

7.17 Hardware and Environmental Factors

Developers often forget the hardware layer:

- Microphone quality — poor capture undermines ASR accuracy.
- Echo cancellation — prevents feedback loops.
- Background noise — use spectral subtraction or beamforming.
- Latency — edge inference or WebAssembly TTS improves response times.

Testing across typical devices ensures consistent accessibility performance.

7.18 Case Study — Conversational Help for Banking

A digital-banking platform introduced a voice assistant for visually-impaired customers. Tasks such as checking balances or transferring funds were handled entirely by voice with MFA security. WCAG compliance rose, and customer satisfaction scores for accessibility jumped 22 points. The assistant used contextual NLP to confirm sensitive actions ("Do you want to transfer £50 to Alex?") before execution, preventing costly errors.

7.19 Developer Checklist

- Implement Web Speech API for browser-based voice control.
- Map voice commands to standard UI actions.
- Announce feedback using ARIA live regions.
- Provide adjustable TTS voices and speeds.
- Store and process voice data ethically.
- Combine voice with other modalities for flexibility.

7.20 Real-World Tools and Frameworks

Voice Accessibility: Tools and Frameworks

Function	Open-Source / API Examples	Notes
Speech Recognition	Mozilla DeepSpeech; OpenAI Whisper; Google Speech API	Whisper excels in noisy environments
Speech Synthesis	ResponsiveVoice; Amazon Polly; Azure TTS	Neural voices with SSML support
Conversational Platform	Rasa; Dialogflow; Botpress	Integrates with REST/GraphQL back ends
Accessibility Testing	aXe Core + speech-simulation scripts	Validates keyboard + voice parity

Developer Takeaway: Prototype quickly with browser APIs, then scale using cloud or hybrid pipelines.

7.21 Future Trends — Emotion, Identity and Multimodality

Next-generation voice systems incorporate emotion recognition, speaker ID, and gesture fusion. Imagine an assistant that notices frustration in tone and simplifies instructions, or a browser that blends gaze tracking with speech input for precision. As standards like WCAG 3 and W3C Voice User Interface (VUI) evolve, these multimodal experiences will define inclusive interaction.

7.22 Limitations of Voice Accessibility

- Public privacy: users may hesitate to speak in shared spaces.
- Speech impairments: AI must recognize atypical articulation—current accuracy remains limited.
- Over-talking: concurrent speech and screen-reader audio can clash.
- Cultural phrasing: idioms vary; intent classifiers must handle diversity.

Testing with real disabled users remains indispensable.

7.23 Developer Takeaways and Best Practices

- Build voice parity, not voice dependency—keep traditional controls.
- Use clear feedback loops for every voice action.
- Design short conversational turns; long monologues reduce comprehension.
- Prefer local inference for sensitive domains (health, finance).

• Document every AI model's limitations and confidence ranges.

7.24 Closing Reflection

Voice interfaces mark a profound shift from accessibility as retrofit to accessibility as interaction design. They restore agency by letting users command technology in their own words. When combined with visual and linguistic intelligence, conversational AI creates truly multimodal experiences—ones that listen, understand, and respond with empathy.

The goal is not to make machines sound human, but to make digital interactions feel humane. As we proceed into the next part—The Architecture of Intelligence—we will examine how these AI capabilities integrate architecturally within front-end and edge infrastructures to sustain performance, privacy, and inclusivity at scale.

Adaptive UI and Dynamic Personalization

8.1 From Static Layouts to Living Interfaces

Traditional front-end design assumes a single visual truth: one layout, one colour scheme, one interaction model. Accessibility frameworks have long encouraged responsive design—adapting to screen size or zoom level—but not to human diversity. Adaptive UI expands that principle. Instead of merely resizing, it personalizes itself to the individual: adjusting typography for dyslexia, spacing for motor stability, or colour palette for low-vision comfort. AI makes such adaptation feasible at scale by learning from behavior rather than assumptions.

8.2 The Logic of Adaptation

An adaptive interface observes, predicts, and adjusts through three continuous loops:

1. **Sensing** — collecting context (device, preferences, behavior).
2. **Reasoning** — inferring user intent or difficulty via ML models.
3. **Responding** — altering presentation or flow without losing meaning.

Adaptive Loops: Signals and Actions

Loop	Example Signals	Adaptive Action
Sensing	Zoom events; colour-scheme preference; motion-reduction setting	Increase text size; switch to dark mode
Reasoning	Slow navigation; repeated mis-clicks	Enlarge targets; extend timeout
Responding	Speech activity detected	Enable voice-first mode; suppress auto-animations

This is accessibility as behavioral intelligence, not hard-coded logic.

8.3 AI-Driven Personalization vs Preference Menus

Most sites still hide accessibility under "Settings → Accessibility". AI replaces toggles with adaptive inference: the system learns what the user prefers through usage.

Example: If a visitor repeatedly increases zoom, the AI stores a preference for larger base fonts. When they return, it pre-applies the setting, silently improving comfort without configuration.

Developer Takeaway: Adaptive AI complements—not replaces—manual controls. Always let users override inferred choices.

8.4 Data Sources for Adaptation

Personalization depends on data, but only ethically sourced signals:

- **Client Settings:** `prefers-color-scheme, prefers-reduced-motion`.
- **Interaction Metrics:** cursor path, dwell time, focus loss.
- **Device Capabilities:** screen size, touch vs keyboard.
- **Voluntary Profiles:** user-saved preferences in local storage.

Avoid covert collection such as eye-tracking or microphone data without consent.

Signal Source, Privacy Level, and Recommended Use

Source	Privacy Level	Recommended Use
OS accessibility APIs	Low risk	Respect existing system settings
Behavioral analytics	Medium	Aggregate only; no personal identifiers
Camera / microphone	High	Use explicit opt-in only

8.5 Personalization Engines in Practice

Modern frameworks (for example, React Adaptive Components, Angular Signals, Next.js Middleware) support conditional rendering based on runtime context. AI layers sit atop these frameworks, feeding context predictions rather than binary flags.

Example flow:

1. Model predicts "user likely low-vision" (confidence 0.82).
2. Context provider sets `theme="highContrast"`.
3. Component library applies contrast variant of tokens.

This pattern externalizes accessibility logic into a context engine, keeping core UI clean and maintainable.

8.6 Machine Learning Models for User Profiling

- **Decision Trees:** fast for binary preferences (e.g., motion vs no motion).
- **Bayesian Models:** estimate probability of preference from observations.
- **Reinforcement Learning:** optimizes interface through reward feedback (e.g., task completion speed).

Edge-based models avoid cloud latency and privacy risks, making personalization real-time and GDPR-compliant.

8.7 Design Systems with Inclusive Variants

Every design token—colour, spacing, animation—should offer an accessible variant. AI engines simply choose which to render.

Token Defaults and Accessible Variants

Token	Default	Accessible Variant
color.text.primary	#333	#000 (high contrast)
motion.transition	ease-in-out 300 ms	None
font.family.base	Helvetica	OpenDyslexic

With tokenized design systems, AI personalization becomes a matter of selecting values rather than injecting CSS patches.

8.8 Real-World Example — Dynamic Contrast Tuning

A media platform deployed an AI contrast model that monitored user scroll behavior. If readers paused frequently or highlighted text, the system inferred contrast difficulty and darkened background incrementally until scroll velocity normalized. Surveys showed a 23% increase in reading-comfort scores without explicit settings.

8.9 Adaptive Typography and Readability

Computer Vision and NLP can collaborate to optimize typography:

- Detect reading speed via scroll pattern.
- Measure fixation time per line (proxied by dwell/scroll cadence).
- Adjust font size or line-height accordingly.

Such micro-adaptations mirror the user's pace and reduce cognitive load—particularly useful for dyslexia or attention disorders.

8.10 Personalization and Cognitive Accessibility

AI can recognize signs of confusion (rapid back-and-forth navigation, re-reading) and simplify interface state:

- Hide advanced options.
- Offer "simple mode".
- Summarize content progressively.

Developer Takeaway: Adaptive cognitive support is most effective when voluntary and reversible. Never trap users in a simplified flow without an exit.

8.11 Ethics of Inference

While adaptive AI improves comfort, it also profiles behavior. Under GDPR and the EU AI Act, developers must provide:

- **Transparency:** explain how preferences are inferred.
- **Consent:** allow opt-in/out of adaptive modes.
- **Data Portability:** export or reset preference profiles.

Accessibility should feel like assistance, not surveillance.

8.12 Integrating with Assistive Technologies

Adaptive UIs must remain compatible with screen readers and keyboard navigation. Dynamic changes should announce via ARIA live regions and respect user focus.

```
<div aria-live="polite">Contrast mode enabled</div
```

Keep animation transitions instant to avoid confusing voice narration.

8.13 Adaptive UI Architecture

A robust architecture includes:

1. **Context Manager** — aggregates signals (device, preferences).

2. **Inference Engine** — predicts user state (vision, motor, cognitive comfort).
3. **Renderer** — applies variants via design tokens and component props.
4. **Feedback Loop** — logs outcomes for model retraining.

Flow: User → Signals → Inference → UI Variant → Interaction → Feedback. This pipeline can run locally within a service worker or server-side for authenticated sessions.

8.14 Developer Workflow Integration

In practice:

- Use React context or a Vue store for adaptive state.
- Expose `<AdaptiveProvider>` to wrap the root layout.
- Register listeners for `prefers-*` media queries.
- Store user consent token in local storage.

By treating adaptation as state, developers gain predictability and debugging control.

8.15 Real-World Example — E-Learning Platform

An education portal implemented adaptive UI for students with varying needs. AI tracked quiz completion time and scroll speed to infer reading difficulty. When detected, the system increased font size, added extra spacing, and offered audio summaries. Engagement rose by 29%, while drop-outs fell by 18%. Accessibility became a competitive advantage, not a compliance cost.

8.16 Performance and Accessibility Trade-Offs

Every adaptive layer adds CPU cost. Optimize by:

- Using Web Workers for background inference.
- Caching preferences locally.
- Deferring model loading until interaction.
- Limiting reflows and DOM mutations.

Measure CLS and LCP to ensure adaptation does not harm performance—the ultimate form of accessibility.

8.17 Standardization and Future Outlook

The W3C Personalization Semantics Module 1.0 defines attributes (for example, `data-purpose`, `data-action`) for AI to map content to user needs.

```
<button data-purpose="checkout">Pay now</button>
```

Assistive tech or AI assistants can translate this purpose into simplified language or an alternative presentation. When widely adopted, these semantics will let AI customize interfaces with precision and consistency.

8.18 Developer Checklist

- Tokenize design variables (colour, spacing, motion).
- Implement a context manager for adaptive state.
- Respect user consent and privacy boundaries.
- Use ARIA live regions for dynamic updates.

• Optimize performance to keep adaptation invisible.

8.19 Closing Reflection

Adaptive UI represents the culmination of everything accessibility strives for: an interface that understands without prejudice. AI enables designs that react to human diversity in real time while preserving choice and control. The accessible web of the future will not be a single view—it will be a living system that meets each person where they are.

Natural Interaction Interfaces

9.1 From Point-and-Click to Human-Centred Interaction

For decades, the web has required translation: humans learn how to speak the computer's language—click here, hover there, fill this field. AI allows the relationship to invert. Natural interaction means computers begin learning our language: gesture, gaze, motion, and emotion. These new modalities—enabled by sensors and machine-learning interpretation—extend accessibility far beyond keyboards and screens. For users who cannot see, touch, or speak in conventional ways, natural interaction becomes liberation rather than novelty.

9.2 Defining Natural Interaction

A natural interface recognizes and responds to human behavior directly, without explicit commands.

Natural Inputs, AI Techniques, and Accessibility Benefits

Input Mode	AI Technique	Accessibility Benefit
Gesture	Pose estimation; skeletal tracking	Enables hands-free navigation for motor-impaired users

Input Mode	AI Technique	Accessibility Benefit
Gaze	Eye-tracking and attention models	Supports users who cannot use their hands or voice
Facial Expression	Emotion recognition	Adjusts difficulty or provides empathetic feedback
Body Movement	Motion classification	Accessible gaming, physiotherapy, and rehabilitation
Touch Pressure / Haptics	Sensor fusion	Detects tremors or substitutes click precision

The web's next accessibility frontier is understanding humans holistically, not just their input devices.

9.3 Gesture Recognition and Motor Accessibility

Computer-vision frameworks such as MediaPipe and TensorFlow.js can interpret body landmarks in real time using standard webcams. By mapping gestures to DOM events, developers can replace mouse actions with physical movement.

Example Flow

1. Detect hand pose via camera.
2. Classify gesture (open palm = scroll, pinch = select).
3. Dispatch synthetic event to interface.

```
if (gesture === "pinch") {
  document.querySelector(".cta").click();
}
```

Developer Takeaway: Gesture control should augment, not replace, standard input. Always maintain keyboard equivalents.

9.4 Eye Tracking and Gaze Interfaces

AI eye-tracking once required expensive hardware; now lightweight convolutional networks estimate gaze from webcams with reasonable accuracy.

- **Hands-free navigation:** dwell to click or look-to-scroll.
- **Adaptive focus:** auto-enlarge text in the region of gaze.
- **Error prediction:** detect fatigue or inattention for cognitive support.

Privacy note: Always request consent before activating gaze tracking; process frames locally to avoid transmitting biometrics.

9.5 Emotion-Aware UX

Emotion-recognition AI analyses facial muscle movements, tone, and syntax to infer affective state. While controversial in marketing, it holds accessibility promise:

- Detect frustration → offer simpler instructions.
- Detect confusion → extend time limits.
- Detect fatigue → suggest rest mode or audio playback.

Combine this with on-device processing for ethical compliance.

9.6 Multisensory Interfaces and Haptics

For deaf-blind or low-vision users, haptic feedback communicates information silently. AI models calibrate haptic patterns to context (for example, short buzz = notification; continuous pulse = error). The W3C Vibration API and emerging WebHaptics API allow browsers to trigger these cues.

Real-World Example
A navigation PWA for blind pedestrians used GPS and computer vision for obstacle detection and transmitted direction cues through smartwatch vibrations—no audio needed.

9.7 Speech and Gesture Fusion

Natural interaction is multimodal. AI lets multiple modes cooperate: a user points while saying "this one," and the system combines speech intent with spatial context. Such fusion relies on timestamp synchronization and probabilistic alignment of sensor streams.

Multimodal Input Pairs and Fusion Logic

Input Pair	Fusion Logic
Speech + Gesture	Word "this" → gesture region → target element
Voice + Eye	Focus target follows spoken object
Gesture + Touch	Stabilizes shaky input for motor impairments

Implementing these on the web can use WebRTC, WebGL, and client-side ML; frameworks like TensorFlow.js and WebNN are closing that gap.

9.8 Cognitive Load Detection

Machine-learning models infer cognitive load from cursor velocity, dwell time, or gaze dispersion. When load spikes, the UI can pause animations, simplify layout, or switch to audio mode.

Developer Takeaway: Always confirm adaptations verbally or visually—silent UI changes risk confusion.

9.9 Ambient Context and Environmental AI

Sensors report brightness, sound, and motion. AI aggregates these into ambient context—the environment around the user.

Signals and Adaptive Actions

Signal	Adaptive Action
Loud noise > threshold	Enable captions; mute autoplay
Low light	Increase contrast; enlarge font size
Device motion = moving	Activate voice-only mode

These features support situational accessibility—helping everyone when conditions temporarily disable them.

9.10 Real-World Example — AI in Virtual Classrooms

An education platform integrated webcam-based attention tracking to assist teachers in online special-education sessions. If students looked away or exhibited frustration, the system suggested activity changes or reading breaks. All data stayed on device. Engagement among neurodiverse learners improved by 32%.

9.11 Edge AI for Latency and Privacy

Natural interfaces demand millisecond responses. Running models on device (WebAssembly, WebGPU, or edge accelerators) ensures speed and privacy. Use model quantization and pruning to fit under ~10 MB for browser deployment. Offload heavy training to cloud; keep inference local.

9.12 Standardization and APIs

- **WebHID API** — connects assistive hardware (eye-trackers, Braille displays).
- **Pointer Events Level 3** — unifies pen, touch, and mouse.
- **WebXR Device API** — supports spatial interaction in AR/VR.
- **Speech Recognition / Synthesis APIs** — for voice integration.

Combining these standards enables adaptive, future-proof experiences.

9.13 Inclusive Design Patterns for Natural Interfaces

1. **Parallel Modality:** provide alternative inputs simultaneously (voice and keyboard).
2. **Progressive Disclosure:** reveal advanced controls when capability is shown.
3. **Feedback Loops:** always acknowledge gestures and speech visibly or audibly.
4. **Calibration:** offer a training step for gesture-recognition accuracy.

Developer Takeaway: "Natural" does not mean intuitive for every-one; teach the system and the user.

9.14 Testing Natural Interfaces

Accessibility QA must evolve beyond keyboard scripts. Use synthetic agents that simulate gestures and voice commands. Gather telemetry on recognition accuracy, latency, and fallback success rate (percentage of times a user needed keyboard backup). A target of > 95% success ensures true equivalence with traditional input.

9.15 Ethical Boundaries and Consent

Cameras and microphones collect intimate data. Ethical implemen-tation requires:

- Explicit opt-in, not implicit activation.
- Local processing first; cloud only with consent.
- Visible indicator when sensors are active.
- Data-expiry policy (automatic deletion after session).

Accessibility must never be an excuse for surveillance.

9.16 Developer Checklist

- Provide multiple input modes (voice, keyboard, gesture).
- Process sensor data locally whenever possible.
- Request and log consent for camera/mic usage.
- Integrate feedback loops for gesture acknowledgement.
- Measure accuracy and fallback rates as core metrics.

9.17 Real-World Example — Accessibility in Public Kiosks

Transport authorities deployed AI-enabled ticket kiosks with gesture and voice control. Users could point to destinations on screen or say them aloud. For wheelchair users unable to reach touch zones, the system auto-adjusted height and zoom. Accessibility audits showed a 70% reduction in assistance requests.

9.18 Challenges and Limitations

- Environmental noise: voice input degrades in public spaces.
- Lighting variance: gesture tracking fails in low light.
- Bandwidth: multisensor streams can strain low-end devices.
- Standardization gaps: browser support is uneven.

Mitigate with graceful fallbacks and progressive enhancement.

9.19 Developer Takeaways Summary

- Natural interaction extends accessibility beyond screens and keyboards.
- AI interprets human signals to enable inclusive control.
- Always prioritize privacy, consent, and fallbacks.
- Measure accuracy and latency like any core UX metric.

9.20 Closing Reflection

The web was born of text and evolved through graphics; its next transformation is human interaction in its purest form. When AI bridges gesture, voice, gaze, and emotion, we move beyond assistive technology to assistive experience. Natural interfaces make the web feel less like software and more like conversation—an environment where technology meets people on their own terms.

Conversational Components and Chat-Driven UX

10.1 The Shift to Conversational Interfaces

W eb interfaces were once transactional—buttons, forms, and menus. Now they are increasingly dialogue-driven. Users expect to type or speak in natural language and receive meaningful responses. Conversational interfaces democratize interaction: they collapse complex navigation into a single chat window and give users—especially those with visual, motor, or cognitive barriers—a frictionless route to their goal. AI-driven chat components represent the next leap for accessibility: interfaces that listen, reason, and respond contextually.

10.2 Conversational UX and Accessibility

Conversational UX (CUX) reframes accessibility from layout to language flow. Instead of designing static pages, developers design conversations that adapt to the user's cognitive and emotional state.

Accessibility Challenges and Conversational Solutions

Accessibility Challenge	Conversational Solution
Complex multi-step forms	Guided chat sequence clarifies one field at a time

Accessibility Challenge	Conversational Solution
Dense navigation	"Ask me anything" shortcut removes visual scanning
Cognitive overload	Context-aware prompts and confirmations
Screen-reader navigation	Linear chat flow mirrors human dialogue

10.3 Components of a Conversational Interface

1. **Input Parser** — captures text or voice and handles spelling errors.
2. **Intent Classifier** — identifies user goals (book appointment, change address).
3. **Dialogue Manager** — keeps context and handles multi-turn logic.
4. **Response Generator** — produces accessible output (text and speech).
5. **Accessibility Layer** — announces updates, manages focus, ensures keyboard parity.

Developer Takeaway: Treat conversational UIs as dynamic forms with strict ARIA and focus control, not chat gimmicks.

10.4 Progressive Enhancement with Chat

Chat should not replace the UI—it should extend it. Provide the same functions through both conversation and conventional elements. If JavaScript fails, users must still complete tasks through normal forms.

This parity maintains WCAG 2.2 SC 4.1.2 ("Name, Role, Value") and prevents accessibility regressions.

10.5 Real-World Example — Accessible Support Chat

A government portal replaced its helpdesk form with an AI-chat assistant. Users typed questions like "How do I renew my driving licence?" The bot parsed intent, fetched relevant steps, and offered a one-click link. Screen-reader users completed queries 40% faster, thanks to structured ARIA live announcements:

```
<div role="status" aria-live="polite">Renewal form ]
```

10.6 Language Models as Accessibility Engines

Large Language Models (LLMs) enable contextual understanding. They interpret natural queries (for example, "show me all accessible PDFs") and convert them into semantic search or API calls.

- Prompt templates for structured replies.
- Function calling for controlled task execution.
- Accessibility guards enforcing safe, concise, WCAG-compliant responses.

Developer Takeaway: Wrap LLMs in strict constraints; never let free-form generation alter live UI without validation.

10.7 Chatbots as Assistive Navigators

Conversational components can act as screen-reader companions. A chatbot can monitor the DOM and offer contextual help: "You are on the payment screen. Would you like me to describe the fields?" Such systems use DOM-diff detection and ARIA role mapping to generate conversational guidance dynamically.

10.8 Cognitive Benefits of Chat-Driven UX

Linear conversation reduces decision fatigue. For neurodiverse users, predictable turn-taking and limited options lower anxiety. AI can vary response speed or verbosity based on comprehension signals—measured through delays, re-reads, or clarification requests. If a user repeatedly asks "What does that mean?", the bot can automatically switch to plain-language mode.

10.9 Integrating Voice and Chat

Voice plus chat unites the strengths of both modalities. The same conversational engine handles both through ASR ↔ NLP ↔ TTS loops.

Developer Tip: Maintain identical state across voice and text channels so the conversation stays synchronized regardless of modality.

10.10 Architecting Conversational Components

Flow: User → Input Parser → NLU → Dialogue Manager → Response Generator → UI Renderer → Screen Reader (with Data APIs / Function Calls feeding the Dialogue Manager).

- Dialogue Manager announces topic changes.
- Renderer updates `aria-live` regions.
- Response Generator limits text length per turn.

10.11 State Management and Memory

Chatbots need short-term memory to remain coherent and long-term logs for analytics. For privacy, store summaries rather than raw transcripts. Apply context windows that forget after N turns or when the task ends, satisfying GDPR minimization.

10.12 Visual and Tactile Chats

Conversation Modalities and Benefits

Mode	Implementation Example	Benefit
Text-Only	<input type="text"> chat window	Simplicity and screen-reader parity
Text + Widgets	Quick-reply buttons	Fewer keystrokes
Speech	Web Speech API	Hands-free interaction
Haptic	Braille display feedback	Inclusivity for deaf-blind users

10.13 Emotional Design in Conversation

Tone matters. AI can detect sentiment and adjust replies—apologetic for errors, encouraging for achievements. In assistive contexts (for example, healthcare or education), this reduces frustration and builds trust.

Real-World Example

An online therapy portal used sentiment-aware chatbots to monitor distress signals and escalate to human counsellors. False-positive rate < 5%, while enabling early, safe interventions.

10.14 Handling Errors and Fallbacks

- "Sorry, I did not understand. You can also use the search bar."
- Keyboard shortcuts to return to main navigation.
- Esc consistently closes chat.

```
<div role="alert">We could not process that reque
```

10.15 Testing Chat Accessibility

- Screen-reader tests (JAWS, NVDA, VoiceOver).
- Keyboard navigation through message history.
- Colour contrast of message bubbles.
- Latency measurement (aim for < 1 s per response).

Record transcripts to evaluate linguistic clarity and avoidance of jargon.

10.16 Security and Privacy in Chatbots

- Encryption in transit (TLS 1.3+).
- Data redaction for PII in logs.
- Clear opt-outs (for example, "Forget my data").
- Session timeouts with confirmation.

Disclose model type and data use in accessible language: "This assistant uses AI to generate replies. No personal data is stored after you leave."

10.17 Ethical Guidelines for Conversational AI

- Explainability: users should know if they are chatting with AI.
- Human escalation: always offer a "talk to a person" route.
- Bias control: audit models for discriminatory language.
- Transparency: provide timestamps and confidence levels in logs.

10.18 Developer Checklist

- Maintain functional parity between chat and UI.
- Announce all dynamic updates with ARIA.
- Store minimal, anonymized conversation data.
- Offer human fallback routes.
- Validate LLM outputs for safety and tone.
- Test chat flows with assistive-tech users.

10.19 Real-World Example — Retail Conversational Shopping

A fashion retailer introduced a chat-driven "Find Your Fit" assistant. Customers typed or spoke "Show me leggings in size 8 navy." The AI parsed colour, size, and category, then filtered catalogue results. VoiceOver and TalkBack users navigated easily because the chat component exposed every message in semantic HTML. Cart conversions rose 17%, while accessibility complaints dropped to near zero.

10.20 Future of Conversational Components

- Detect when the user is lost and proactively offer help.
- Generate summaries of long articles ("Would you like a 1-minute recap?").
- Translate live text into simplified language.

Conversational components will evolve into ubiquitous assistants—always present, respectful, and inclusive.

10.21 Closing Reflection

Chat is the universal interface: everyone, regardless of ability, understands conversation. By integrating AI dialogue systems thoughtfully—with semantic structure, clear feedback, and ethical transparency—developers transform accessibility from compliance into companionship. When a website can talk and listen with empathy, the web itself becomes conversational—a medium where information feels shared, not merely delivered.

AI for Accessibility and Inclusivity

11.1 Beyond Compliance: Inclusion as a Design Principle

Accessibility often begins as a legal requirement; inclusivity turns it into a design philosophy. Artificial Intelligence gives developers the tools to bake inclusion into every layer of product creation, from discovery and prototyping to deployment and feedback. Where compliance ensures access, AI ensures belonging—interfaces that not only function for everyone but feel designed for everyone.

11.2 The Spectrum of Inclusivity

Inclusivity extends beyond permanent disability to encompass situational and cultural diversity:

Dimensions, Example Barriers, and AI Solutions

Dimension	Example Barrier	AI Solution
Physical	Limited mobility or dexterity	Gesture, voice, and adaptive UI controls
Sensory	Visual or auditory loss	Computer vision and speech interfaces

Dimension	Example Barrier	AI Solution
Cognitive	Dyslexia, ADHD, autism	NLP simplification and predictive guidance
Cultural / Linguistic	Idiomatic or language bias	Multilingual translation and tone adaptation
Situational	Sun glare, noise, time pressure	Context-aware dynamic adjustment

AI makes these adaptations responsive rather than static, recognizing diversity as normal, not exceptional.

11.3 AI as an Inclusion Catalyst

AI enhances inclusion in three ways:

1. **Detection** — identifying exclusion patterns hidden in data (for example, voice models that misunderstand certain accents).
2. **Generation** — creating alternative representations (captions, summaries, translations).
3. **Adaptation** — personalizing experience based on real-time context.

These three axes form a feedback loop: the system learns from every interaction to become more inclusive over time.

11.4 Inclusive Design Powered by AI

AI bridges the gap between inclusive intent and execution by automating laborious tasks and surfacing invisible biases.

Design Phase: Traditional Approach vs AI Assist

Design Phase	Traditional Approach	AI Assist
Ideation	Manual persona creation	Data-driven, inclusive personas reflecting diverse abilities
Wireframing	Static mock-ups	Adaptive prototypes that simulate low-vision or colour-blind modes
Copywriting	Manual reading-level checks	NLP that rephrases for clarity and tone
Testing	Limited user pool	Synthetic assistive user agents testing dozens of variations

Developer Takeaway: Use AI early—in design and content—to prevent exclusion, not patch it after launch.

11.5 Detecting Bias and Disparity

Machine learning can reveal where products serve some groups better than others. Examples include voice assistants misrecognizing female voices in noisy rooms, chatbots trained on ableist language, or vision models that mislabel assistive devices.

Bias-auditing pipelines measure performance variance across demographics and report inequities in accuracy, latency, or error rate.

Remediation Cycle

1. Detect bias

2. Diagnose root cause
3. Retrain with balanced data
4. Validate with diverse testers

Inclusivity requires continuous iteration, not a one-time fix.

11.6 Inclusive Datasets and Model Training

- Source datasets across cultures, genders, and abilities.
- Include assistive-tech interaction data (screen-reader events, voice variations).
- Apply data augmentation for rare cases (for example, synthetic speech impairments).
- Document limitations through Model Cards and Data Statements.

Developer Takeaway: Diversity in training data is accessibility at source.

11.7 Inclusive AI Content Generation

AI content systems can produce multiple formats simultaneously:

- Plain-language summary
- Audio version
- Captioned video
- Screen-reader-optimized HTML

This "one-prompt, many-outputs" approach ensures content equity without duplicating effort. CMS pipelines can orchestrate TTS and ASR APIs to automate generation.

11.8 Real-World Example — Inclusive News Platform

A public-service broadcaster used AI to translate breaking-news articles into easy-read language and audio summaries in ten languages. Usage among screen-reader users rose by 61%, and average time on page increased by 40%.

11.9 Inclusive Localization and Translation

Machine translation often misses cultural nuance. Localization engines with contextual embeddings and tone control ensure translated content respects social norms and reading difficulty (for example, using polite forms in Japanese or simplifying for children's sites). Accessibility is not just about language—it is about politeness, tone, and cultural comfort.

11.10 AI in Inclusive Testing

AI can synthesize user personas that simulate different disabilities and backgrounds, then run flows (checkout, registration) automatically.

Metrics to Track

- Success rate per persona
- Error types (visual, cognitive, motor)
- Frustration events (abandoned flows, retries)

These analytics quantify inclusive performance for continuous improvement.

11.11 Intersectionality and Compound Accessibility

Real users rarely fit neat categories. Multi-label profiling can represent intersections and trigger combined supports—for example, text simplification plus font enlargement and audio summary for a user with age-related sight loss and mild dyslexia.

11.12 Corporate Inclusion Dashboards

AI aggregates data from support tickets, usage logs, and surveys to produce dashboards tracking:

- Accessibility defect rate
- Inclusive feature adoption
- Assistive-tech session counts
- Sentiment scores from diverse audiences

11.13 AI for Inclusive Recruitment and Workflows

- NLP analyses job adverts for gender-coded phrases.
- Video-meeting AI adds real-time captioning.
- Scheduling bots avoid over-booking outside accessible hours.

An inclusive product starts with an inclusive process.

11.14 AI and Social Equity

AI can lower digital entry barriers: voice-first interfaces support limited literacy; low-bandwidth compression keeps tools usable in developing regions. Community-driven datasets democratize benefits globally.

11.15 Governance and Regulation

New regulations set standards for transparency and risk classification. Developers should:

- Register high-risk accessibility systems where applicable.
- Maintain auditable logs of AI decisions.
- Provide accessible explanations for model outputs (for example, "why this caption").

Governance is a framework for trust.

11.16 Real-World Example — Accessible Banking Assistant

A bank deployed an AI assistant combining speech recognition, text simplification, and gesture support. It adapted interface density based on stress detected from voice tone. Contact-center load for accessibility queries fell 45%, and customer trust scores rose 20%. Transparency features included live explanations of AI actions: "I am simplifying your dashboard to reduce distraction."

11.17 Ethical Boundaries and Empathy

AI can simulate understanding, but only humans embody empathy. Ethical inclusion requires humans in the loop to review tone, context, and consequences. Design with disabled people, not merely for them—participatory AI and co-created datasets are the gold standard.

11.18 Developer Checklist

- Audit models for bias and performance variance.
- Use inclusive, diverse training datasets.
- Document model limitations and confidence levels.
- Embed inclusive AI content generation in your CMS.
- Apply governance and consent principles (privacy by design).
- Test intersectional user journeys, not isolated scenarios.

11.19 The Economic and Moral Case

Inclusive products reach broader audiences, improve SEO, and reduce litigation risk. Beyond profit, inclusive AI helps balance information inequality—every adaptive caption, translation, or voice prompt is a micro-act of equity.

11.20 Closing Reflection

AI is neither inherently inclusive nor exclusive—it reflects its makers. Built with diversity in mind, it becomes the greatest ally of accessibility since the web's inception. Inclusivity is no longer a department; it is an architecture. By combining data, ethics, and empathy, developers can turn AI from automation into understanding—a web that not only works for everyone but with everyone.

Governance and Risk in
Intelligent Accessibility

12.1 Why Governance Matters

A I offers extraordinary promise for accessibility—adaptive inter-faces, real-time captions, personalized comprehension. But every line of automation introduces a line of accountability. Who verifies the fairness of models that decide what users see? Who ensures accessibility data is not repurposed for surveillance or profiling? Governance transforms innovation into responsibility. Without it, "intelligent accessibility" can quietly become "intelligent exclusion".

12.2 Defining Governance in AI Accessibility

Governance is the framework that ensures accessibility systems are:

- **Transparent** — decisions can be explained in plain language.
- **Accountable** — humans remain responsible for AI outcomes.
- **Auditable** — logs exist to trace decisions and training data.
- **Inclusive** — diverse voices guide design and evaluation.
- **Compliant** — systems adhere to law and ethical standards.

Governance bridges design ethics and legal obligation. It does not stifle creativity—it scaffolds trust.

12.3 Risk Categories in Intelligent Accessibility

Key Risk Types, Impacts, and Mitigations

Risk Type	Example	Impact	Mitigation
Algorithmic Bias	Captioning AI misinterprets accented speech	Exclusion; discrimination	Diverse datasets; bias audits
Data Privacy	Adaptive UI stores disability profile	Unauthorized disclosure	On-device inference; consent and anonymization
Automation Overreach	AI overrides user settings	Loss of autonomy	Human override; transparency controls
Regulatory Non-Compliance	Unverifiable model decisions	Legal penalty	Documented explainability and traceability
Security Vulnerability	Assistive APIs expose telemetry	Exploitation	Encryption; access controls; monitoring

12.4 The Human-in-the-Loop Principle

AI accessibility tools must assist, not replace, human judgment. The "human-in-the-loop" model ensures:

1. **Verification:** humans validate AI suggestions before deployment.
2. **Intervention:** users can override adaptive behavior.

3. **Escalation:** ethical concerns can be raised and resolved.

12.5 Accountability Chain

Roles and Responsibilities

Role	Responsibility
Accessibility Lead	Ensures compliance and inclusive design direction
Data Scientist	Documents datasets and bias mitigation
Product Owner	Balances innovation with regulatory risk
Legal / Compliance	Verifies adherence to data and disability law
Ethics Board	Oversees fairness, transparency, consent
Developer	Implements privacy-safe, explainable features

12.6 Regulatory Landscape

- WCAG 2.2 / 3.0 — digital accessibility criteria.
- GDPR (Europe) — personal data and profiling.
- EU AI Act — risk classification and transparency.
- U.K. Equality Act (2010) — prohibits digital discrimination.
- ADA Title III (U.S.) — accessible online services.
- ISO/IEC 42001 — emerging AI management standard.

12.7 AI Risk Classification for Accessibility Systems

The EU AI Act introduces tiers: unacceptable, high, limited, and minimal risk. Most accessibility AI trends toward **high risk** because errors can restrict equal access—demanding documentation, traceability, and human oversight.

12.8 Privacy by Design

- Collect only essential signals.
- Perform inference locally where feasible.
- Use pseudonymized identifiers.
- Encrypt telemetry in transit and at rest.
- Set retention limits and provide deletion options.

A user should never have to trade privacy for inclusion.

12.9 Transparency and Explainability

Users deserve to know why AI behaves as it does. Example in UI:

```
Contrast adjusted automatically based on your syst
```

Model cards should summarize: purpose and scope; dataset provenance; evaluation metrics; known limitations; and a responsible contact.

12.10 Documentation and Traceability

- Version history — model iterations and data updates.

- Validation logs — accuracy, fairness, and usability results.
- Decision mapping — links between predictions and UI actions.

Traceability enables root-cause analysis when regressions occur.

12.11 Ethical Review Boards

- Review datasets for representational balance.
- Approve adaptive features that alter UI.
- Audit privacy safeguards and opt-out mechanisms.
- Publish annual transparency reports.

Boards should include disabled experts, not only ethicists and executives.

12.12 Testing for Governance Compliance

- **Bias testing:** check variance in accuracy across demographics.
- **Explainability tests:** confirm users understand adaptive behaviors.
- **Accountability mapping:** verify ownership for each automated decision.
- **Incident simulation:** rehearse response to AI misbehavior or data breach.

Accessibility testing now includes *trust testing*.

12.13 Incident Response Framework

1. **Detection:** monitoring flags abnormal behavior.
2. **Containment:** disable or roll back features.
3. **Communication:** notify users and regulators promptly.

4. **Investigation:** document root cause transparently.

5. **Remediation:** retrain models, update policy, publish outcomes.

12.14 Accessibility Model Lifecycle

Lifecycle Phases and Governance Focus

Phase	Governance Focus
Data Gathering	Representation; consent; privacy
Training	Bias mitigation; documentation
Validation	Accuracy; fairness; usability
Deployment	Monitoring; version control
Post-release	Feedback; retraining; audit

Continuous governance mirrors continuous integration—both prevent rot.

12.15 The Role of Tooling

- Model-card generators to auto-document metadata.
- Ethics-linting to scan for missing disclosures.
- Governance dashboards to visualize risk levels.
- Explainability APIs (for example, LIME, SHAP) to make behavior transparent.

AI can help keep AI accountable.

12.16 Organizational Policy Integration

- Embed policy into SDLC gates.

- Add vendor clauses for accessible, explainable AI.
- Train employees on ethics, privacy, inclusion.
- Set procurement criteria for bias-tested datasets.

12.17 Real-World Example — Responsible Personalization

A retail platform deployed AI personalization that adjusted layout density for users with motor impairments. After privacy review, inference ran locally and a transparency toggle appeared: "Adaptive layout enabled. Turn off." Satisfaction increased 38%, complaints fell, and regulators commended the privacy-first approach.

12.18 International Collaboration

Cross-border alliances (GPAI, OECD AI Principles, W3C Ethical Web AI Community Group) support consistency, credibility, and early influence on evolving standards.

12.19 Developer Checklist

- Map accountability for each AI component.
- Adopt privacy-by-design and on-device inference.
- Maintain model cards and data statements.
- Implement explainability messages in UI.
- Establish an ethics board with disabled representation.
- Simulate incident responses annually.
- Audit and retrain models continuously.

12.20 Closing Reflection

Intelligent accessibility promises autonomy, equality, and empathy—but only under governance that values people above performance. When organizations document, disclose, and involve, AI becomes not only compliant but compassionate. Governance is the quiet architecture of trust—the invisible framework that keeps innovation humane.

Partnership with Disability Communities

13.1 From Consultation to Collaboration

Accessibility projects have often treated people with disabilities as test subjects rather than design partners. Artificial Intelligence now magnifies that imbalance: models trained on incomplete data can reproduce exclusion faster than any human team. Real progress demands co-creation—embedding lived experience into every stage of AI development. True partnership means moving beyond "user testing" to shared authorship of datasets, interfaces, and evaluation frameworks.

Developer Takeaway: Inclusion begins before code is written. Engage disabled contributors when defining the problem, not only when verifying the solution.

13.2 Why Lived Experience Matters to AI

AI systems learn patterns, not empathy. Without direct input from disabled people, those patterns mirror mainstream assumptions about sight, hearing, cognition, or mobility. Lived experience provides nuance that data alone cannot:

- What "usable" means when keyboard navigation is your lifeline.
- How "intuitive" differs for screen-reader users.

- Why small interaction delays can mean independence or frustration.

Collaborating with communities supplies ground-truth data and ethical calibration, ensuring that intelligence reflects reality rather than convenience.

13.3 Models Built with the Community

Community Roles Across the AI Lifecycle

Stage	Community Role	Outcome
Data Collection	Contribute voice, image, or interaction samples	Balanced datasets
Model Validation	Evaluate real-world performance	Bias detection
Interface Design	Co-create adaptive components	Practical usability

Community collaboration transforms AI from speculation into representation.

13.4 Design Research with Dignity

Participatory design must respect autonomy and privacy. Good practice includes:

- Accessible consent forms in plain language and multiple formats.
- Fair compensation for participants' time and expertise.
- Feedback loops so contributors see how insights influence outcomes.

- Anonymized storage of data with the right to withdraw.

Accessibility is ethical only when participation itself is accessible.

13.5 Building Ethical Data Pipelines

AI relies on examples. If those examples exclude disabled voices, bias is inevitable. To correct this, teams should:

- Include accessibility metadata (for example, assistive-tech usage) in training logs.
- Maintain diversity manifests listing representation across disability types.
- Conduct bias audits on model predictions.
- Publish data statements documenting scope and limitations.

Transparency converts potential exploitation into shared stewardship.

13.6 Community Advisory Boards

Establishing a Disability Advisory Board ensures long-term governance. Boards typically include:

- Representatives from disability organizations.
- Academics specializing in inclusive design.
- Disabled technologists with lived technical expertise.

Responsibilities: review datasets, test new features, approve ethical use cases, and provide continual accountability. This institutionalizes empathy.

13.7 Case Study — AI Captioning Done Right

A media-streaming company partnered with deaf and hard-of-hearing consultants to train its captioning AI. Instead of outsourcing generic datasets, it recorded community-approved samples of accents, ambient noise, and slang. The result: 30% fewer transcription errors and higher satisfaction ratings among users. Partnership replaced assumption with authenticity.

13.8 Co-Designing Assistive Tools

AI opens opportunities for user-driven innovation. Blind developers contribute to computer-vision projects, autistic designers refine cognitive-support tools, and people with limited mobility shape gesture-recognition systems. By embedding contributors directly in development teams, organizations gain insight that no empathy map can match.

Developer Takeaway: Hire inclusion, do not simulate it. Diversity inside the team outperforms diversity "in persona".

13.9 Communication and Transparency

Community trust depends on clear, honest communication:

- Explain how AI features work and what data they use.
- Share success metrics and known limitations.
- Invite public feedback through accessible channels (email, chat, captioned calls).

Transparency transforms risk into relationship.

13.10 Long-Term Engagement Strategies

Partnerships must persist beyond project cycles. Sustainable engagement includes:

- Annual community reviews of AI performance.
- Open-data contributions back to disability research repositories.
- Joint hackathons or accessibility challenges.
- Mentorship pipelines bringing disabled students into tech roles.

These actions convert consultation into capacity-building.

13.11 Balancing Representation and Privacy

Capturing diverse data risks exposing sensitive information. Mitigation principles:

- Collect only what is necessary for model accuracy.
- Use synthetic or obfuscated data when possible.
- Implement differential privacy and secure enclaves.
- Offer transparency reports showing data-handling policies.

Ethical AI protects the people it learns from.

13.12 Integrating Community Feedback into Releases

Feedback must translate into action. Establish formal mechanisms:

1. Tag community-raised issues in JIRA or GitHub.
2. Assign clear owners and deadlines.

3. Report resolutions publicly.

Closing the loop validates that participation drives real outcomes.

13.13 Education and Mutual Learning

Developers learn from lived experience; communities learn about emerging technologies. Workshops, webinars, and co-training build shared literacy: understanding model bias, data rights, and adaptive design possibilities. Mutual education transforms empathy into expertise.

13.14 Community-Led Evaluation Metrics

Disabled testers often propose metrics beyond compliance—comfort, trust, autonomy. AI measurement frameworks can incorporate these qualitative signals using sentiment analysis or satisfaction surveys. Quantifying feelings keeps human well-being central to machine performance.

13.15 The Economics of Partnership

Compensating participants fairly is non-negotiable. Budget for:

- Paid community consulting hours.
- Accessibility review stipends.
- Travel or remote-access accommodations.

Investment in authentic insight prevents the far greater cost of reputational damage and biased systems.

13.16 Collaboration Platforms and Tools

Practical collaboration benefits from accessible infrastructure:

- Shared design systems in Figma or Adobe XD with screen-reader support.
- Issue-tracking tools with semantic labelling and ARIA-compliant navigation.
- Video-conference platforms offering live captions and transcripts.

When the process is inclusive, the product follows suit.

13.17 Policy and Governance Alignment

Government and corporate accessibility mandates increasingly expect community involvement. Document partnerships within equality-impact assessments and AI governance reports. Compliance achieved through collaboration carries greater credibility than checkbox audits.

13.18 Real-World Example — Smart Mobility Partnership

A transport authority developing an AI-powered journey planner collaborated with wheelchair users and visually-impaired commuters. Their insights shaped route-ranking algorithms to prioritize step-free access and real-time lift status. Post-launch, satisfaction among disabled travelers rose 54%.

Co-design turned policy into progress.

13.19 Challenges and Mitigations

Common Challenges and Practical Mitigations

Challenge	Mitigation
Tokenism (symbolic consultation)	Formalize advisory roles with decision power
Participation fatigue	Rotate contributors and respect capacity
Accessibility of tools	Use platforms tested with assistive tech
Resource constraints	Embed inclusion costs into project budgets

Acknowledging challenges demonstrates maturity, not weakness.

13.20 Developer Checklist

- Involve disabled people from project inception.
- Compensate and credit contributors.
- Maintain transparent communication channels.
- Use ethical, privacy-preserving data practices.
- Integrate feedback into release cycles.
- Document partnerships for accountability.

13.21 Closing Reflection

AI gives us unprecedented reach—but reach without representation is regression. By partnering with disability communities, developers ensure that intelligence grows from understanding, not assumption. The most inclusive systems will not be those that guess what users need, but those built *with* users who already know. Collaboration, not computation, is the true architecture of intelligent accessibility.

Measuring & Maintaining Intelligent Accessibility

14.1 Why Measurement Matters

In software, what we measure defines what we value. For years, accessibility measurement has relied on static checklists—success criteria met or failed, percentages of WCAG conformance achieved. But intelligent systems require a new vocabulary. When AI powers adaptation and automation, accessibility becomes fluid. It evolves with context, data, and user behavior. The question is no longer "Is the site accessible?" but "Is accessibility performing optimally for every user, in every condition?" To answer that, teams need metrics that are as dynamic as the experiences they create.

14.2 From Compliance to Continuous Intelligence

Traditional audits operate as snapshots; intelligent accessibility demands streams. Treat accessibility like performance monitoring—continuous, contextual, and outcome-based.

Traditional vs Intelligent Accessibility

Traditional Approach	Intelligent Approach
Binary pass/fail checks	Continuous scoring and adaptation

Traditional Approach	Intelligent Approach
Manual audits	Automated telemetry and predictive alerts
Single-device testing	Multimodal and situational testing
Human QA after release	Integrated accessibility observability

This shift turns accessibility into a living metric, monitored and optimized alongside performance and security.

14.3 Defining New Metrics

AI enables experience-level measurement—evaluating whether semantics and adaptations actually work for people in practice. Example metrics include:

- **Assistive Success Rate (ASR):** percentage of interactions completed via assistive technology.
- **Adaptation Latency:** time from signal (for example, prefers-contrast) to UI change.
- **Comprehension Confidence:** AI-estimated likelihood that content was understood.
- **Personalization Accuracy:** precision of adaptive features against user preferences.
- **Inclusion Coverage:** proportion of personas or disability categories served.

These complement traditional metrics (for example, Lighthouse accessibility score) to reflect inclusive performance.

14.4 The Accessibility Telemetry Pipeline

1. **Signal Collection:** capture screen-reader events, keyboard focus maps, accessibility API calls.
2. **Normalization:** clean and anonymize data to protect privacy.
3. **Model Inference:** infer satisfaction, fatigue, or confusion patterns.
4. **Dashboard Visualization:** present live analytics to engineers and stakeholders.
5. **Feedback Loop:** feed outcomes back into design and model retraining.

Developer Takeaway: Treat accessibility events as first-class telemetry—signals to be understood, not noise to be filtered.

14.5 Continuous Accessibility Integration

Embed measurement inside CI/CD so every commit runs automated scans, visual regression for contrast, and AI-based content analysis.

Example workflow: Commit → Build → AI Accessibility Scan → Model Inference → Report / Block Merge. If predicted regression risk ≥ 0.75, pause the merge for review.

14.6 The Role of Synthetic Users

Synthetic users—simulated personas using reinforcement learning—navigate with virtual screen readers, voice commands, and keyboards to generate scaled data (for example, time to task completion, error recovery rate). They discover issues beyond scripted paths.

14.7 Accessibility Scorecards and AI Governance

Accessibility Scorecard (weights are illustrative)

Dimension	Source	Weight (%)
Technical Compliance	Automated + manual	30
Functional Usability	AI observation + user testing	30
Cognitive Simplicity	NLP readability models	20
Adaptive Responsiveness	Model latency + success rate	10
Ethical Transparency	Governance audit	10

An aggregate **Intelligent Accessibility Index (IAI)** can benchmark releases quarterly.

14.8 Predictive Accessibility

Train models on historical incidents to flag likely regressions (for example, new color tokens or complex JS patterns associated with past failures). Shift from reactive fixes to proactive quality engineering.

14.9 Balancing Automation with Human Judgment

Metrics quantify; humans contextualize. Blend dashboards with regular sessions involving disabled participants to interpret tone, trust, and comfort.

14.10 Case Study — Continuous Accessibility at Scale

A global education platform added a real-time AI monitor to its front end. Each deployment audited color contrast, alt-text relevance, and ARIA completeness, streaming results across 12 regions. Over six months:

- Accessibility regressions dropped by 67%.
- Issue triage time decreased by 45%.
- Manual audit frequency halved.

Automation empowered, rather than replaced, the accessibility team.

14.11 Feedback Loops and Model Retraining

Use reviewer corrections to update models (for example, reclassifying a false positive on ARIA roles). Keep pace with evolving frameworks, browsers, and AT.

14.12 Ethical Measurement

- Collect minimal data.
- Always anonymize.
- Offer explicit opt-in.
- Provide visibility into how accessibility data is used.

Transparency turns measurement from intrusion into collaboration.

14.13 Integrating Accessibility KPIs into Business Metrics

- Percentage of releases meeting the IAI threshold.
- Support ticket reduction attributable to accessibility improvements.
- Conversion uplift from adaptive design.
- Customer satisfaction among assistive-tech users.

When accessibility moves revenue, retention, and reputation, it earns a durable roadmap slot.

14.14 Cross-Functional Collaboration

Create an *Accessibility Insights Board* to review metrics and AI reports in sprint ceremonies. Accessibility becomes everyone's metric.

14.15 Maintaining Accessibility Debt Logs

Track accessibility debt like technical debt—prioritize by impact, not count. Use clustering to group similar defects, estimate remediation effort, and visualize trendlines.

Developer Takeaway: Debt is best managed when visible, quantified, and tied to outcomes.

14.16 Tools and Frameworks

- Deque axe-core with AI extensions for real-time audits.
- Evinced for accessibility observability.
- Google Lighthouse CI with ML-based risk prediction.
- Microsoft Accessibility Insights with telemetry APIs.
- Custom TensorFlow.js models for NLP readability scoring.

Orchestrate these in DevOps to maintain continuous assurance.

14.17 Future of Accessibility Analytics

Browsers may expose native accessibility telemetry APIs for real-time comfort analysis (contrast, motion, latency). WCAG 3.0 scoring will likely incorporate adaptive metrics and machine-assisted evaluation that reflect actual outcomes.

14.18 Developer Checklist

- Instrument accessibility events as first-class telemetry.
- Establish an Intelligent Accessibility Index (IAI).
- Use synthetic users for scaled testing.
- Integrate predictive audits in CI/CD.
- Apply ethical data practices (consent, anonymization).
- Report accessibility KPIs alongside performance metrics.

14.19 Closing Reflection

Accessibility is no longer a static audit item; it is a living performance layer. AI transforms it into a continuous dialogue between systems and users. What was once measured in checkboxes will be measured in comfort, comprehension, and confidence—the true markers of intelligent accessibility: progress that never stops learning.

The Future of Inclusive AI Design

15.1 A Turning Point

The convergence of AI and accessibility marks a historic inflection in digital design. Where accessibility once meant retrofitting compliance, intelligent systems now enable anticipatory inclusion—interfaces that sense, adapt, and evolve alongside users. The next decade will decide whether AI becomes an instrument of empowerment or an engine of exclusion. The difference will depend on how designers, developers, and policymakers embed inclusivity into algorithms themselves.

15.2 From Automation to Augmentation

The 2020s witnessed AI automate routine testing and content adaptation. The 2030s will shift toward augmentation—AI amplifying human accessibility work, not replacing it.

Today vs Emerging Future

Today	Emerging Future
Automated audit bots	AI assistants collaborating with designers in real time
Static captions	Context-aware, multilingual live captioning

Today	Emerging Future
Keyboard focus testing	Predictive cognitive-load estimation
WCAG compliance	Adaptive, outcome-based accessibility metrics

Automation closes gaps; augmentation elevates experience.

15.3 Adaptive Semantics and WCAG 3.0

The forthcoming WCAG 3.0 (W3C Silver project) embraces outcome scoring over binary pass/fail rules. AI will underpin this by interpreting semantics dynamically—measuring readability, navigation ease, and error recovery empirically. Expect browsers to ship with built-in AI assessors producing real-time accessibility telemetry, creating self-healing feedback loops between development and use.

15.4 Inclusive Design as Default

Accessibility will cease to be a bolt-on. Design systems will embed inclusion primitives—ARIA roles, adaptable tokens, cognitive hints—as defaults. AI models trained on inclusive datasets will enforce these automatically during design linting.

Developer Takeaway: "Inclusive by design" must become as non-negotiable as "responsive by design".

15.5 Universal Multimodality

The future interface is multimodal by nature. Touch, voice, gesture, gaze, and text coexist fluidly. AI fusion engines will infer user context and prioritize the optimal channel. Example: a user starts browsing via voice while cooking; the AI shifts to haptic alerts when the environment grows noisy. Such seamless modality blending will become foundational to UX.

15.6 Edge and Federated Intelligence

Privacy concerns will drive intelligence to the edge. Federated learning enables models to train on-device, sharing only gradients, not personal data. This architecture supports accessibility personalization without surveillance, satisfying GDPR and AI Act requirements.

Real-World Example: A health-app consortium uses federated models to improve voice accessibility for speech-impaired users without ever transmitting raw recordings.

15.7 Contextual AI and Environmental Inclusion

Next-generation systems will factor ambient conditions—light, noise, motion—to deliver situational accessibility. Rather than relying on manual "dark mode" toggles, the UI will adapt to sun glare automatically. Contextual AI turns accessibility from a static state into a continuous environmental negotiation.

15.8 Synthetic Testers and Simulated Users

Testing will evolve from manual audits to fleets of synthetic users powered by reinforcement learning. They will emulate screen-reader interactions, voice commands, and cognitive limitations, generating telemetry across thousands of flows. This approach scales real-world variability into every build pipeline.

15.9 AI and Inclusive Creativity

Generative AI will reshape inclusive storytelling—auto-producing images with balanced representation, voices without bias, and language that resonates across cultures. Developers should fine-tune these models on diverse datasets and expose provenance metadata for transparency, for example:

```
<meta name="ai-origin" content="synthetic" />
```

15.10 Predictive Accessibility Analytics

Accessibility analytics will mature into predictive governance. Dashboards will flag not only current defects but future risks: "High probability of contrast regression in upcoming theme release." Machine-learning pipelines trained on historical sprints will estimate accessibility-debt trajectories and suggest preventive actions.

15.11 AI Co-Design with Disabled Creators

Future AI systems will be co-trained with disabled designers, writers, and testers, embedding lived experience into algorithms. Participatory datasets and open benchmarking will ensure that AI learns empathy rather than approximates it.

Developer Takeaway: Inclusion cannot be reverse-engineered; it must be co-authored.

15.12 Global Regulation and Ethical Frameworks

Expect harmonized global policies—EU AI Act, potential U.S. ADA AI addenda, and a U.K. Equality AI Code of Practice—mandating risk classification and explainability. AI systems affecting accessibility will require human-audit trails and fairness proofs. Ethics becomes engineering.

15.13 The Role of Open Source

Open-source projects (for example, axe-core AI, TensorFlow accessibility models, Inclusive Components libraries) will anchor community trust. Transparency enables peer review and collaborative improvement, spreading inclusion through shared innovation.

15.14 Real-World Example — Smart City Accessibility

A European smart-city project integrates pedestrian cameras, weather sensors, and AI path-planning to guide blind citizens safely through dynamic streetscapes. The system adjusts routes for rain, construction, or crowds in real time—accessibility as civic infrastructure.

15.15 Emerging Technologies to Watch

Technologies with Inclusive Potential

Domain	Inclusive Potential
Neural Interfaces	Direct control for users with paralysis
Digital Twins	Simulated accessibility testing across environments
Quantum AI	Complex optimization for multi-factor adaptation
Synthetic Media Watermarking	Authenticity and trust in generated assistive content

15.16 The Human Frontier

AI can amplify empathy but not originate it. The future of inclusive design lies in human governance: multidisciplinary teams blending data science, UX, psychology, and lived experience. When every sprint includes disabled voices, AI learns to design with people, not for them.

15.17 Developer Checklist

- Prototype adaptive, multimodal components.
- Implement federated learning for privacy-safe personalization.
- Integrate predictive analytics for accessibility debt.
- Publish model cards for transparency.
- Collaborate with disabled co-designers.

15.18 Closing Reflection

The future of inclusive AI design is not about smarter algorithms but kinder architectures—systems that value dignity as much as efficiency. Technology's greatest achievement will be empathy at scale.

Building an AI-Ready Accessibility Culture

16.1 Culture Before Code

S ustainable accessibility begins with mindset, not tooling. An AI-ready culture equips every team—engineers, designers, and product owners—with the literacy to understand, question, and responsibly deploy intelligent systems. Without that culture, even the best models reinforce bias or indifference.

16.2 Defining AI Literacy for Accessibility Teams

AI literacy means knowing enough to:

- Evaluate model limitations.
- Interpret confidence scores.
- Understand privacy implications.
- Communicate AI decisions in plain language.

Training accessibility teams in these areas ensures they remain custodians of ethics, not mere consumers of automation.

16.3 Organizational Readiness Matrix

AI Accessibility Readiness Levels

Maturity Stage	Characteristics	Next Step
Reactive	Accessibility as compliance; AI viewed skeptically	Establish inclusive governance board
Transitional	Some automation, limited policy	Define AI usage guidelines and risk matrix
Adaptive	Cross-disciplinary AI-a11y projects	Integrate AI ethics into design reviews
Transformative	AI-driven inclusion strategy organization-wide	Continuous learning and community contribution

16.4 Governance and Accountability

Set up an **AI Accessibility Council** that includes engineers, disabled staff, legal experts, data ethicists, and UX researchers. Responsibilities:

- Approve model usage, audit datasets, and track incident reports.
- Publish transparent documentation (model cards, data sheets).

Accountability transforms ethics from slogan to system.

16.5 Upskilling and Continuous Learning

Provide ongoing training on:

- WCAG 3.0 outcomes.
- AI model basics and bias mitigation.
- Accessibility testing with intelligent agents.
- Privacy and consent frameworks.

Certify internal "AI Accessibility Champions" who guide peers and review releases.

16.6 Tooling Ecosystem Integration

1. **Version Control Hooks:** run accessibility AI scans on commit.
2. **CI/CD Stages:** integrate predictive linting.
3. **Analytics Dashboards:** track inclusive metrics alongside performance.

AI becomes invisible infrastructure rather than a separate initiative.

16.7 Cross-Functional Collaboration

AI-ally culture thrives where silos collapse:

- Designers inform data scientists about human contexts.
- Developers translate ethical policies into code.
- QA shares telemetry with UX for continuous feedback.

Weekly "inclusion stand-ups" align teams on both values and metrics.

16.8 Inclusive Procurement and Vendor Management

Third-party AI services can re-introduce bias. Procurement contracts must mandate:

- Accessibility conformance reports (VPAT 2.4 + AI supplement).
- Transparent training data sources.
- Opt-out mechanisms for users.

Inclusion extends down the supply chain.

16.9 Measurement and Success Metrics

Accessibility Culture Measurement Framework

Metric Type	Example Measure
Quantitative	% pages passing AI accessibility audit; model accuracy per persona
Qualitative	User satisfaction among disabled testers; empathy survey scores
Operational	Number of AI recommendations reviewed by humans
Ethical	Incidents of model bias or privacy breaches

Publish metrics quarterly to maintain transparency.

16.10 Reward and Recognition

Celebrate inclusive innovation through:

- Accessibility leaderboards.
- Hackathons on AI-a11y features.
- Awards for empathetic UX solutions.

Recognition nurtures pride and momentum, embedding inclusion in identity.

16.11 Communication and Transparency

Explain AI features clearly in public documentation:

"Our personalization engine adapts colour contrast using on-device AI. No personal data leaves your browser."

Plain-language disclosure transforms anxiety into trust.

16.12 Ethical Incident Response

When AI fails—misclassifying a user or producing biased content—treat it as a security incident. Define protocols for:

- Immediate rollback or disablement.
- Public statement template.
- Root-cause AI analysis.
- Corrective data retraining.

Transparency is protection.

16.13 Partnership with Disability Communities

Build formal alliances with advocacy groups and charities. Offer co-design programs, paid testing partnerships, and data sharing with consent. This ensures lived experience shapes every release cycle.

16.14 Leadership and Vision

Executives must speak the language of inclusion. Set OKRs linking revenue, retention, and accessibility KPIs. Vision statements should pair innovation with empathy:

> "We will lead in ethical AI by designing technology that listens, learns, and includes."

16.15 Global Knowledge Exchange

Encourage open publication of findings—whitepapers, conference talks, GitHub examples—so the community advances collectively. Accessibility is strengthened by collaboration, not competition.

16.16 Future-Proofing the Culture

As AI evolves, culture must adapt. Establish feedback rituals: retrospectives focused on inclusion debt, quarterly AI ethics reviews, and continuing-education stipends. A living culture keeps accessibility aligned with technological progress.

16.17 Developer Checklist

- Create an AI Accessibility Council.
- Train cross-functional teams in AI ethics and WCAG 3.0.
- Integrate AI audits into CI/CD.
- Mandate accessibility clauses in vendor contracts.
- Publish transparent metrics and incident reports.
- Reward inclusive innovation publicly.

16.18 Closing Reflection

Building an AI-ready accessibility culture is less about algorithms than accountability. When empathy becomes an organizational reflex, AI naturally aligns with human values. The next era of digital inclusion will not depend on a single model or framework but on the collective discipline of teams that choose transparency, diversity, and continuous learning. Accessibility, once a checklist, becomes a shared creed—and with that creed, AI fulfils its promise not to replace human understanding, but to extend it.

Disclaimer

This publication is intended for educational and informational purposes only. It does not constitute legal advice, professional consultancy, or formal accessibility certification guidance.

While every effort has been made to ensure accuracy and relevance at the time of publication, web standards, accessibility regulations, and AI technologies evolve rapidly. Readers and organizations are encouraged to consult qualified legal, compliance, or accessibility professionals before making decisions based on the material presented in this book.

Neither the author nor the publisher shall be held liable for any direct, indirect, incidental, or consequential damages resulting from the use of, or reliance upon, the information contained herein.

By reading this book, you acknowledge that it is intended solely as a learning resource to promote awareness, critical thinking, and independent research into the responsible application of artificial intelligence for accessibility and inclusion.

Ashok Kumar Yadav is a UI Engineering Leader, accessibility specialist, and advocate for inclusive digital experiences. With extensive expertise in developing global e-commerce and enterprise platforms, he bridges the intersection of AI-driven innovation and human-centered design, ensuring technology serves everyone—regardless of ability, context, or language.

Throughout his career, Ashok has led and contributed to large-scale initiatives involving Salesforce Commerce Cloud (SFCC), WCAG and ARIA standards, and AI-powered accessibility testing. He collaborates closely with UX, QA, and architecture teams to design adaptive systems that emphasize clarity, equity, and performance.

An active member of the accessibility and AI ethics communities, Ashok writes and speaks on the future of practical inclusion—where design meets empathy and automation amplifies awareness.

He believes the next era of development will be not only intelligent but profoundly inclusive. Based in Texas, USA, Ashok continues to contribute to open-source accessibility projects and mentor professionals worldwide.

www.ingramcontent.com/pod-product-compliance
Lightning Source LLC
Chambersburg PA
CBHW071423210326

41597CB00020B/3628